Praise for The Marriage Makeover: Finding Happiness in Imperfect Harmony ships. . . . And it offers the astounding idea that having a marriage characterized by such 'imperfect harmony' can be part of a satisfying, happy life."

—from the Foreword by Julia M. Lewis, Ph.D., coauthor with Judith S. Wallerstein, Ph.D., and Sandra Blakeslee, of *The Unexpected Legacy of Divorce*

"I recommend this book to all married individuals who wish to maintain the stability of their unions and protect the well-being of their children. This book is a major contribution to the healing of our fractured system of marriage."

—Paul R. Amato, Professor of Sociology, Demography, and Family Studies, Pennsylvania State University

The Lazy Husband

How to Get Men to Do More Parenting and Housework

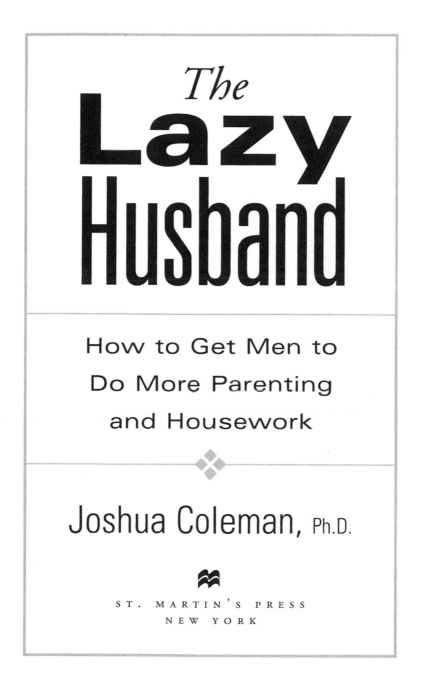

Joshua Coleman, Ph.D.

ST. MARTIN'S PRESS
NEW YORK

www.stmartins.com

BOOK DESIGN BY DEBORAH KERNER/
DANCING BEARS DESIGN

ISBN 0-312-32794-3
EAN 978-0312-32794-1

10   9   8   7   6   5   4   3   2

To **Ellie,**

FOR ALL OF THE OBVIOUS REASONS . . .

Contents

Acknowledgments

This book was brought to life by many people. I would first like to thank my hardworking agent, Felicia Eth, for finding a good home for my book at St. Martin's. It's great to have you in my corner. To my editor at St Martin's, Elizabeth Bewley, for your warmth, clarity, and insight. Thanks for your attention to detail and to the big picture. It was a great pleasure to work with you. To Heather Jackson for your interest and belief in the project.

There are many, many writers, researchers, and teachers whose writings influenced this book. While I don't have space to name them all (beyond the copious endnotes), several deserve an additional acknowledgment. Sociologist Arlie Hochschild's book, *The Second Shift*, provided a wellspring of original thought, social research, and analysis to draw from. My book was inspired by a wish to address many of the issues raised in her groundbreaking book. Sociologist Scott Coltrane's *Family Man: Fatherhood, Housework, and Gender Equity* was a rich source of historical and contemporary analysis about the complexities of gender, and how ideas about gender affect men's and women's views about parenting and housework. Economist Rhona Mahony's book, *Kidding Ourselves: Breadwinning, Babies, and Bargaining Power,* taught me how economics and game theory can be used to think about bargaining, power, and communication in marriage. Many of the how-tos of my book were influenced by her ideas. Sociologist Jay Belsky's book, *The Transition to Parenthood: How a First Child Changes a Marriage: Why Some Couples Grow Closer Together and Others Apart,* provided countless insights into the enormous ways that couples are changed by the arrival of a first child. Finally Ann Crittenden's *The Price of Motherhood: Why the Most Important Job in the World Is Still the Least Valued* was a rich resource for the many ways that our society and others undervalue women's contributions to their children, their home, and to the economy.

My book was also made stronger by the generous reading and critiques of my friends and colleagues. They are, in alphabetical order, Kenny Bender, Jessica Broitman, Christie Carlson, Claudette Coleman, Jessica Flynn, Lori Katzburg, Lisa Levine, Janice Levine, Metece Riccio, Michael Simon, Heidi Swillinger, Katherine Vincent, and Jean Weaver.

I would like to thank my friends for their friendship. It means everything.

I am blessed with three great children, Misha, Max, and Daniel. You are a source of tremendous joy.

To my parents, Steve and Corinne, for showing me that love, commitment, and a long-lasting marriage can be fun. Additonal thanks to my father, a former columnist, for his reading of the manuscript.

To my brothers, Adam and Mitch, for being great brothers to me.

Finally, to my wife, Ellie, who served as book widow, coleague, editor, friend, and partner. For all of those times I wanted to be a lazy husband, and you wouldn't let me.

The
Lazy
Husband

Introduction

They say that you should write about what you know, and I know all about being a lazy husband. My laziness once stretched, like the British Empire, from the small villages of my children's toys and bottles to the teeming civilizations of dirty laundry, food to be prepared, kids to be played with, and kitchens to be cleaned. I developed advanced techniques to avoid work and prided myself in their execution. I feigned exhaustion when the grass began to grow so wild that my children could hide in the yard and the fire department couldn't find them. I developed allergies to all household cleaning agents, especially anything that could ever be used on a toilet, run through a washing machine, or poured on a kitchen floor. My laziness was a work of art, a lifestyle happening, an inspiration to all of my (male) friends.

And then, over time, something terrible happened. My wife began to change. Not as in screaming, crying, guilt-tripping change. But as in, "Okay, Jack, game is over. I am no longer pulling my weight and yours in this household." I was concerned. So I tested her limits just the way the raptors did in the first *Jurassic Park* movie by hurling themselves against the side of the cage. She didn't flinch.

I tried acute, hysterical sensory loss such as

Memory failure: "I never agreed to take out the garbage *every* week!"
Hearing failure: "You never said I should change their diapers more than once a day!" and
Loss of vision: "Actually, I *don't* see any dust balls."

It took a while for me to realize that my lazy days were drawing to a close, and that a new era of greater participation was setting in. My wife was becoming someone that I couldn't shrug off, scare off, or bug off. She was someone that I had to reckon with.

✦

As a psychologist and self-help author, I often receive desperate pleas from mothers wanting to know how to get their husbands to be more involved with the housework and children. Some women are on the verge of divorce, while others are still struggling to comprehend why her partner acts like a '50s-style uninvolved guy when he promised to share 50 percent of the parenting and housework before the children came on the scene.

I believe that the onus is on men to do the changing. However I don't think they're going to be in any rush because the current system works so well for them. So, unfortunately, if we're going to get your husband to do his fair share, you're going to have to lead the charge here and that's what this book is about.[1] I could write a book like this for men, detailing all of the ways that they should pitch in more equitably, and touting the benefits that they'd gain, but I prefer to write books that will be read. If I wrote a book like this for men, it would be the wives who would buy it for their husbands, and that would only worsen the problem because it would sit unopened along-side titles like *Parenting During Your Infant's First Year, How You Can Save Your Marriage,* and *Let's Talk About Feelings.* In other words, women will have to lead the charge on this because men won't.

However, while this book is written for women, they're not the only ones who will benefit by it. Your husband and children will also gain from making your house a place where everything doesn't get dumped on you. For example, consider the follow-ing facts from social science research:

➤ Women with partners who are actively involved in parenting and housework are happier and more satis-fied with their marriages.[2]

➤ Women who do the majority of housework and child care in a family are more prone to physical illness and more likely to become depressed.[3]

➤ Children score higher on academic tests in homes where dad is more involved.[4]

➤ When children are raised in homes where dad isn't in-volved in housework, boys are often more anxious at three and a half, and girls are less warm and less task oriented.[5]

➤ School-age children who do housework with their fa-thers have more friends at school, and are more likely to get along well with others. They're also less likely to disobey teachers.[6]

➤ Women are far more likely to think about divorce when they're married to men who neglect the house and kids.[7]

➤ Men who regularly do housework are associated with wives who are more interested in sex.[8]

➤ Children who do housework with fathers are less likely to be socially withdrawn or suffer from depression.[9]

Why Should You Read *The Lazy Husband*?

This book was inspired by the mothers in my practice, conversations with my women friends and colleagues, my own marriage, and the letters I receive on a regular basis from stressed-out moms. The ideas found here are based on my clinical experience, as well as my readings in the areas of psychology, sociology, anthropology, women's studies, and economics. My central goal in writing *The Lazy Husband* is to help you understand how to motivate your mate to be a better partner to you, and a better father to your children.

Since the book is written for you, we'll look at what you may have to change in yourself in order to enact changes in your partner. We'll discuss how society's messages about being a woman and mother may inhibit your bargaining power or position of authority in the household. As a way to understand how your belief systems affect you and your partner, we'll examine traditional marriages, egalitarian marriages, and marriages that are somewhere in between. We'll see how your experiences in childhood helped or hindered your capacity to be sufficiently entitled and assertive with your husband, how children changed your marriage for better and for worse, and how understanding those changes can prepare you to create a better reality. We'll look at different types of husbands and wives as a way to gain insight into the strengths and obstacles that each personality type produces. We'll explore common differences between the sexes and see how those play out in your relationship.[10] Finally, we'll give your husband his very own chapter for how he can contribute to your happiness and increase the peace in the household. In other words, this book will take a big, bold look at how you can do less by getting your husband to do more.

· 1 ·

The Perfect Mother

Most of the adults of my generation were raised in some version of a "children should be seen and not heard" era. Boy, have times have changed. Contemporary children are growing up in an environment where children should be seen, talked to, validated, encouraged, supported, and developed. They have gone from being quietly kept in the background to being loudly and proudly paraded into the foreground. In many households, it's the *parents* who are seen and not heard, and children are the axis upon which the household turns.

My wife and I were as guilty of this as any contemporary parent. When our children were young, our living room looked like a display center for a Toys-Я-Us outlet. LEGO sets and Lincoln Log constructions dotted the floor like an architectural layout for a dilapidated shopping center. Our refrigerator was transformed into a display case for finger paintings and doily cutouts. Spellings and misspellings of words from multicolored magnetic plastic alphabets competed with macaroni-and-paste compositions of turkeys, flowers, and semideranged faces. And that was just the front. The side was, and remains, a freestanding magnet-reinforced album of their three lives starting from birth to the present, gradually occupying more and more space until every time we put a new picture up, an avalanche of history risks cascading to the floor.

The New Era of the Child

O ur culture's shift toward children's well-being has dramatically affected our identity as men and women, husbands and wives, mothers and fathers. At the same time, changes in the economy, marriage, and divorce have created confusion and turmoil about who's supposed to do what with the house and the kids. This chapter will examine the many ways in which the burden of these changes has fallen onto women's shoulders, and what may need to change in your household for your partner to do more, and for you to do less.

✦

W e are today cursed and blessed by an unprecedented amount of information that *any* parent can now get at *any* time to answer *any* question they could ever have about *any* of their children. Internet Web sites, newspaper articles, and whole sections of bookstores are dedicated to serving this eager and anxious population. Magazines with titles such as *Child, Parenting, Pregnancy, Pregnancy and Baby, Babytalk, TWINS, Mommy Too,* and *Working Mother,* to name a few, testify to this insatiable parenting market.

On the one hand, this increase in information and awareness has relieved suffering for millions of families. For example, the relatively recent ability to pinpoint such problems as learning disabilities, attention deficit disorder, Asperger's syndrome, and countless other psychological and educational disabilities has positively changed the lives of millions of adults and their children. In addition, easy-to-access information has made the sometimes heartbreaking and confusing journey of parenting a far less brambled path.

However, with education comes guilt and fear of doing the dreaded "wrong thing." As parents, we're terrified of blowing it. A distraught mother recently said to me, "Last night I lost my patience with my two-year-old and bawled him out for the first time. I don't usually do that, but I'm worried that I scarred him for life." Worry that some small parental loss of control will result in long-term damage is a common concern that I hear on a daily basis in my psychotherapy practice.

Homework and After-School Activities

Residents of the United States currently hold first place for working more hours than any other nation,[1] and we now appear to be moving our children in the same direction. As job security and long-term financial security seem less and less assured, schoolwork and grade performance are more important than ever. As a result, many parents are exhausted not only from jobs, housework, and parenting but from their children's homework and the hundreds of activities in which many children are involved. Parents whose children are in public schools have to work increasingly hard to make sure that their children get an adequate education, while also worrying about their physical safety.[2] Wealthier parents are moving their children to private schools as the public schools worsen every year from a lack of funding for teachers and educational supplies.

This increased emphasis on a hands-on education means more and more work for overwhelmed parents as they try to lessen the load for their overwhelmed children. Playing has been replaced with play dates, free time has been replaced with structured time, hanging out in the neighborhood until dark has been replaced by hanging out in the neighborhood under the watchful eyes of kidnap-wary adults.[3]

Our view of parenthood has also been changed by the fact that many parents of today have gone through their own psychotherapy and gained a thorough understanding of the ways that their parents harmed, neglected, or mistreated them. As a result, they know firsthand the damage that can be done through parental errors, and feel terrified that they'll hurt their children in the same way that they felt hurt by their parents. Knowing the mistakes of their parents may cause them to be fiercely committed to be the kind of parent that they never had. Unfortunately, many pursue this entirely noble task at the costs to their own health[4] and the health of their marriages.

While men are hardly immune to these worries, women are bearing the major brunt of this child emphasis. This is because this increased consciousness occurs at a time when, among other things, mothers are less likely than ever to have the time, resources, and energy to do what they would like to be good mothers. While women now have unprecedented opportunities to enter the workforce and to establish meaningful and rewarding careers, many feel torn by the division of loyalties they feel between their children's needs and their needs to support their families or to maintain outside interests.[5]

Paradoxically, this new cultural emphasis on children occurs at a time when our society's commitment to parents is lower than it's been in decades.[6] More and more employers are demanding workloads and schedules that create chaos for families, and introduce even greater obstacles to maintaining healthy and intact marriages. Studies show that parents who have to work night shifts or rotating shifts have a greater likelihood of divorcing than those with more stable schedules.[7] Because at least half of today's marriages will end in divorce, women and men feel an increased sense of worry and insecurity about whether their particular family will still be together in the next month, year, or decade. Many become preoccupied with their children because it's the one stable relationship that they can expect to have in the future.[8]

Changing Boundaries

As our view of childhood has changed, so has our view of parenting changed in recent decades. From the 1920s to the 1970s, Americans steadily shifted their child-rearing emphasis from valuing conformity, church loyalty, and obedience to focusing on children's autonomy, tolerance, and the ability to think for themselves. This change was accompanied by a transformation in the family climate from an authoritarian to a more democratic and permissive one.[9] As a result of these developments, the boundaries between adulthood and childhood began to blur.

For example, when I was growing up, I couldn't stand my parents' music, clothing, and a few of their friends. I would no sooner have put on a Bing Crosby record than they would have worn a tie-dyed T-shirt, smoked a bong, or waxed poetic about the intensity of a Jimi Hendrix solo. They were the *adults*—foreign, unfathomable, living in a world I scarcely deigned to penetrate except to get the keys to the car.

However, when my daughter became a teenager, I knew precisely which pile of clothes and books to dig through if I couldn't find something from my CD collection. Her choice of clothing in adolescence was not too different from what I might have worn as a teen; thrift-store chic. In addition, I relied on her to tell me who was new and interesting to listen to (since most of my friends think that anything written after 1972 is an abomination before the rock gods of our generation).

As with parental education, this blurring of generational boundaries has had many benefits. My daughter, now a young adult, discusses her life with me in a way that I wouldn't have dreamed of doing with my parents. However, this blurring makes many parents confused about what distinguishes a harmful from a helpful application of parental authority. Studies show that the most effective parents are *authoritative*.[10] Authoritative parents are defined as being affectionate and loving with their children, but strong in their ability to set limits and make demands. Authoritative parents are contrasted with *authoritarians,* who are highly controlling and show little affection or tenderness toward their children. They're also contrasted with *permissive* parents, who are loving and affectionate but unable to set appropriate limits. Both *authoritarian* and *permissive* parents are less likely to raise well-adjusted children than *authoritatives*.

While earlier generations of parents were more likely to err on the side of being authoritarian, today's parents seem more likely to make errors of permissiveness.[11] For example, many mothers feel a lot of guilt about being away from their children to work outside the home. As a result, it's not uncommon for them to have a hard time setting appropriate limits when they're home because they worry that they're already hurting their kids with their absence.

A mother recently came to my office wanting advice about how to deal with the anxiety of Chloe, her nine-year-old daughter.* Over several meetings with the parents and child, it became clear that Chloe was anxious because her parents were so worried about making a mistake that they refused to provide guidance for her. They allowed her to yell at them and to make parental decisions such as when she would go to bed and what she would eat.

Chloe's anxiety stemmed from a feeling that she was stronger than her parents, and that no one was big enough to watch over her. Both of Chloe's parents worked long hours in their careers, and felt guilty about spending so much time away from her. As a result, they worried that setting normal limits were unfair, given how much time they were already gone.

This dynamic is much like the one that I see with divorced dads in my practice. Because they have so little time together, it pains them to see their children upset in the inevitable ways that occur with limit setting. As a result, they don't set the limits that their children sometimes need.[12] Many of today's stressed-out, guilt-ridden, full-time parents make the same mistake due to a similar kind of guilt and anxiety.

---

*All names and details have been changed to protect client confidentiality.

Losing Time

Sadly, our worry about our children getting enough time with us causes many parents, mothers in particular to create time for them by giving up on time for themselves. Whether it's a decrease in sleep, hobbies, or a social life, women, more than men, pay for time by decreasing the amount spent on other personal needs and interests.[13]

> **GWEN:** *When I was growing up my mother worked hard but she had one job and that was being a homemaker. She had plenty of time with us because that was her occupation. If I want to get time with my girls, I have to make sacrifices somewhere; less sleep, less time with my friends, less time for relaxation, whatever. I used to play tennis, work out, do yoga, whatever—but since I've become a mother, I just feel so selfish taking time for myself. It isn't even that I want to spend every waking second with them. It's more like I feel like if I don't, it means I'm a terrible mother.*

The other area where women create time for their children is by giving up time with their husbands. A recent poll showed that couples now spend far fewer hours together than they did just twenty years ago.[14] Some parents allow their children to sleep with them from infancy onward, in part, because they feel so deprived of time with them during the day. While there may be good reasons for a "family bed,"[15] it's not always a decision that benefits a marriage.[16]

This is because a mother's anxiety about her child can override her concern about her husband's needs to also have her attention. There's a saying that goes, "A man gains a child and loses a wife." Many men feel hurt and rejected by the central focus that a child gains in his wife's life. Men who feel displaced, hurt, rejected, or devalued by the arrival of a child are more likely to retreat from doing housework or parenting. Their "laziness" is a protest for feeling displaced and unimportant.[17]

> BILL: *Since Hank was born last year we don't do anything together without him, including sleep. I'm crazy about the little guy, but I feel like I've fallen off the map in terms of Debby's interest. It's not just sex, it's like he's become everything and the marriage isn't that big of a priority to her.*

Parental Boredom

Today's mothers are also compromised by messages that parenting should be a source of ongoing fulfillment. The reality is that parenting can be boring, frustrating, anxiety provoking, and infuriating. Researchers Linda Thompson and Alexis Walker[18] found that while around one-third of mothers find parenting fun and meaningful, another third don't find it that meaningful or enjoyable, and the remaining third have pretty mixed feelings about it. Messages that mothering should be a source of endless fulfillment create guilt, anxiety, and shame for women who don't feel particularly thrilled by their role.

Men, on the other hand, understand parental boredom and frustration all too clearly. They also experience relatively little conflict over those realities. Their ability to prioritize and pursue activities that they enjoyed prior to becoming parents may be one of the reasons that their stress levels out much sooner than mothers after the birth of a child.[19] Because fathering doesn't play such a central role in a man's identity,[20] few feel as many pangs of conscience when they're bored, annoyed, or unfulfilled by being dads. Women, on the other hand, are more likely to see this as a personal flaw in them as women.[21]

> CLARISSA: *I hate talking to my sister about parenting because she makes me feel so inadequate. She always talks about how* wonderful *it is being a mother and how* fulfilling *it is, and I just don't feel that way. Maybe someday I'll get into this whole maternal-bliss thing, but right now I just feel stressed out and exhausted. I sometimes wonder if something is wrong with me that I don't feel more excited about being a mom.*

Gender

Our experience of ourselves as male or female is something that's created and affirmed on a daily basis through our work, our families, and our relationships.[22] Part of women's relative passion about parenting over men's has to do with the way in which mothering is more central to women's identities. While many men take pride in their children, their homes, and in their abilities as fathers, they less commonly experience those activities as fundamentally central to their identity and self-esteem.[23]

Social expectations about what men and women do play out in the housework realm. For example, a single man who lives alone and is a slob is commonplace. Anna Quindlen's statement that most men live like "bears with furniture"[24] is an affectionate testimony to this. People aren't surprised when single men are slobs, yet few blame a messy house on a husband once men get married. A woman who lives alone and keeps her apartment like a pigsty is more likely to be viewed in a critical way by both men *and* women. In fact, women do even *more* housework when they marry and men do even *less*.[25]

This gender difference also plays out in expectations of what men and women do or don't do as parents. For example, few would look at a child who went to school with peanut butter on his face and dirty clothes and wonder, *What was this father thinking?* Despite our culture's drift toward more involved dads, mothers are still seen as the primary caretaker of the house and child. This perspective that "mom's in charge" means that women who aren't as involved in maintaining their homes or kids are far more likely to be censored by a society that tells her that it damned well *is* her job to care. In other words, women's identities are more influenced by house and children, in part, because others are more likely to judge them by those yardsticks.

Interestingly, the idea that moms are to blame for a child's behavior hasn't always been the case in the United States. Before the industrial revolution, fathers were considered the authorities on raising children, and therefore received the blame or credit for how well their kids turned out. It wasn't until the nineteenth century that the blame began to shift to women as a "cult of domesticity" evolved, instructing women that their place was in the home.[26]

While there have been important changes since then, the belief that home and parenting are women's work persists into the present, and causes many women to feel unentitled to make demands of a fair exchange for all of the work that they do with their house and kids.[27] As author Ann Crittenden writes in *The Price of Motherhood: Why the Most Important Job in the World Is Still the Least Valued,* the myth that men "support" their families prevents many women from seeing themselves as valuable economic players and equal partners. She notes that it's hard to feel cheated of the fruits of your labor if you don't believe that what you're doing is labor.[28]

Let's take an example. Robert earns thirty dollars an hour as a mechanic while his wife earns fifteen dollars an hour as a librarian at the state university. They both believe that she should do more at home because her time is not as "valuable" as his. While this is true in the marketplace, that calculus only makes sense if raising children is considered unimportant. Mothers who buy in to the marketplace argument of parenting begin their negotiations from a far weaker position than those who see their contributions to their children, their marriage, and their husbands as priceless.

Who's Got the Power?

Historically, women have entered marriage with far less power than men. Until the middle of the nineteenth century, women didn't have the right to own their own property in the United States, and had no legal say in family matters, including determining how money would be spent when it was earned through their own labor. When a woman became a widow, her husband's estate was passed on to his heirs, and it was up to them to provide for her.[29]

In 1848 this began to change with the passage of the Married Women's Property Act permitting married women to hold property and to gain protection from their husband's debts if they became widowed. This act later gave them the right to share joint custody and to an equal inheritance with their children in the case of divorce.[30] However, it wasn't until 1880 that a married woman could obtain property without her husband's consent, or use legal recourse if he mismanaged their property or shared assets.[31]

Jobs and Motherhood

Women's wages have been well below those of men up until the recent past. For example, from 1930 to 1980, the earnings of full-time working women were only 60 percent of men's earnings. This gap narrowed dramatically in the 1980s and early 1990s, though an earning gap of at least 20 percent has persisted for the past twenty years.[32] Despite these gains, when women become mothers, their power and bargaining position decreases because their financial power typically decreases.[33] This is because women who take more than a brief maternity leave are punished by being taken off the fast track to promotions and career advancements.

This decrease in financial stability also makes women who become mothers more dependent on their husbands. Those who prided themselves on their independence prior to childbirth may suddenly find themselves in the uncomfortable position of needing financial and emotional support from their husbands in new and unexpected ways. Among other reactions, this may raise unresolved anxieties from childhood about needing help and not having it be forthcoming.

Many couples begin to experience problems for the first time when a child comes on the scene because both members have to newly navigate this shift in roles and responsibilities. This may explain why a majority of couples experience a big decrease in marital satisfaction after the arrival of children.[34] While a woman may experience an increase in stress and a decrease in power, a man may feel burdened by the increase in financial obligations, especially if his wife doesn't go back to work. In addition, men who enjoyed their wife's independence and activity level prior to children may feel burdened by her expressions of dependence or anxiety after a child arrives.

GERRY: *Before our kids were born, Shauna and I did everything together. We went hiking, bike riding, river rafting. It was a really adventurous, romantic life. I had never met a woman like her who was so independent and strong. That all changed when she became a mother. Now it seems like she worries about everything and whatever activities we did together have pretty much ground to a halt. It drives me crazy!*

SHAUNA: *We had a blast before kids, but I feel like Gerry hasn't made the shift into being a dad. It's like he still wants to spend as much time doing all of the things we used to do and ignore the fact that we have to cut back on our expenses and other things. Besides, since I've become a mother, I don't feel as big a need to always be out doing things. I'm happy to*

*hang out with the kids. It feels like he wants to pretend we
don't even have children.*

Compared to What?

S tudies on families reveal something surprising: when
women are trying to determine what's fair to expect from
their husbands, they don't compare themselves with what their
husbands are doing; they compare themselves to what other
women are doing. This causes both men and women to accept a
standard of participation from the husband that is problematic
for the wife.[35] Both men and women are also hampered by the
lack of role models to navigate this new domestic order. When
women look to their own mothers for examples, a majority find
someone who did the majority, if not the entirety, of the parenting and housework. Recalling what their fathers contributed
doesn't provide much guidance because, in all likelihood, he had
his feet propped up before and after dinner, and was out with his
friends on the weekends. This lack of models is one reason why
women continue to carry the second shift despite its unfairness.

What Are the Husbands Thinking?

W hile many men recognize that their wives are doing
more, and may even feel guilty about it,[36] they also
look at other men's behavior to help them figure out what's fair.
In addition, they look at their own fathers and come up looking
good in comparison.

> JACK: *I don't recall my father doing anything around the house growing up. I mean, he'd work in the yard and fix things, but I think my brothers and I were pretty much my mother's responsibility. And I definitely never saw him do laundry, mop a floor, or cook a meal with the exception of the occasional Sunday barbeque. Compared to my father, I work my butt off and my wife* still *complains about me!*

What men don't factor in is that their wives are also doing a lot more than *their* mothers ever did, and usually with bigger financial and social demands. In addition, while men's roles have changed a bit in the past thirty years, women's have changed *enormously*.[37] Sociologist Arlie Hochschild found that men who did the most family work were those that had the most *distant* relationships with their fathers.[38] This is probably because these men were the least interested in using their fathers as role models, and the most motivated to distance themselves from them. Men who are close to their fathers may behave more like them because of the guilt, loss, or sadness they would feel if they behave too differently from them.

Gatekeeping

While many guys use their wives' standards as an excuse to get out of work, some mothers create or participate in the creation of a Lazy Husband by *gatekeeping* the quality and quantity of his involvement. Gatekeeping is a term that sociologists use to explain how much a spouse allows the other spouse to participate in some activity such as parenting, housework, or managing the finances. People often gatekeep by complaining about the other's standards, by redoing tasks, or by refusing the other's offer to help.[39]

Women's gatekeeping can occur for many reasons. Some women gatekeep as a way to prevent their partners from butting into an arena where they enjoy a sense of authority.[40] This may be taking care of the family's needs, or ensuring that the house and parenting are maintained to a certain standard. While gatekeeping is common in traditional households, it can also occur in homes where both parents believe that the parenting and housework should be shared equally.[41] It commonly occurs when women feel guilty or inadequate sharing a role that they saw their mothers perform without a man's involvement.[42]

> **EVELYN**: *I just don't feel right making Rick do as much housework as I do. I know we both work full-time but my mother would have never let my father do the laundry or wash dishes. It just doesn't feel right to me.*

Gatekeeping is an important behavior to understand because the ambivalence that generates it causes many women to be manipulated or warned off by their husbands' excuses or rationales. It may also make them less likely to assert themselves when they need to. A common reason why women gatekeep around housework is because they don't like how their partner cleans—*if* he cleans! This difference in standards is a frequent battle in many homes.

> **PAUL**: *Harriet thinks I'm a slob and I don't think that's fair. I don't keep the house immaculate, but that doesn't make me*

a slob. I also only have so many hours in a day and if I get a free hour the last thing I'm going to do is spend it cleaning. Besides, whenever I do clean she just goes over what I did anyway, so why bother?

Similarly, a mother might gatekeep a father's parenting out of a fear that he'll do it wrong. As a result, he doesn't get a chance to learn on his own.

JEFF: *I pretty much feel like whatever way I parent it's the wrong way for Michelle. "Watch out for his neck!" "You know, it's a lot faster if you lift up his legs with one hand and put the diaper under him with the other." "That's not the kind of baby food he likes." I'm starting to feel like, "Fine. You want it done your way, be my guest!"*

This isn't to say that men are the innocent victims of women's cruel and heartless gatekeeping behavior. Many men ensure that they won't have to do family work by maintaining low standards, forcing their wives to act as managers, acting incompetent, waiting to be nagged, or doing the tasks far less frequently than their wives would like.[43] Sometimes a man's lack of participation has less to do with his partner's gatekeeping than with his unwillingness to get involved under *any* circumstances. These are all important themes that we'll talk about in upcoming chapters. Because, whether your partner is uninvolved as a result of your being overly involved or uninvolved because he's a stubborn dude, you'll need a new set of behaviors and strategies to create change in your house and marriage. And that's where we turn next.

· 2 ·

Creating Change

I t's important to think strategically if you're going to get your husband to stop being lazy. While thinking strategically occurs at both the conscious and unconscious levels, you will get more out of him by becoming *acutely aware* of what each of you has with which to bargain. I say each of you because it's not only important to know what cards you have in your hand but also which ones your partner holds and is willing to play.

While we all wish that love were a place of unconditional approval and acceptance, real-life marriage doesn't work that way. The reality is that each of us constantly evaluates whether we're getting as much out of the bargain as the other. When we are getting enough, our needs to strategize and negotiate recede into the background and a kind of harmony is achieved. When we're not, we have to reexamine what we're getting, what we're not, and how we're gonna go and get it.

Women often feel more guilty engaging in this kind of hard-boiled, strategic thinking in marriage because they're socialized to be more empathic and self-sacrificing. In this chapter we'll delve more into the attitudes and behaviors that you'll need in order to get your husband to do more. I'll show you advanced techniques in bartering and negotiation, and how you can use your strengths in the marriage to gain influence with your husband.

The Problem with Motherhood

The person who cares the most often has the least bargaining power. As economist Rhona Mahony writes, the head start of attachment that women gain by carrying an infant through nine months of pregnancy may predispose them to less bargaining power because of their greater relative investment in the child.[1] For example, after an infant arrives, most women feel a strong sense of attachment almost immediately. This is aided by hormones triggered by nursing such as prolactin and oxytocin, endocrine connectors that men don't have in the same quantities to bond them to the child.[2] It's no small wonder that women feel a sense of personal authority and propriety over their children; biologically, they feel connected to the child in a way that a man may never know, especially during its infancy.[3]

Let's take Karen and Carl. Karen gave birth last month to a healthy boy. While Carl is obviously infatuated with the baby, he doesn't respond nearly as frequently to the baby's crying as does Karen. He prefers to take a wait-and-see approach. Karen, on the other hand, gets up at the first sign of distress. Her attitude is, "Why wait until the baby is really upset?" How does this affect who will do what? It probably goes something like this. If Karen wants Carl to respond as quickly, she has to:

➤ convince Carl of its importance to her, or
➤ convince Carl of its importance to the baby, or

> ➤ persuade Carl that whatever other activity he's in-
> volved in is less important than attending to the baby
> at that moment.

As you can see, Carl potentially has more bargaining power in this situation because he's not as strongly motivated by the baby's discomfort. Karen has less power because she's *highly* motivated by the baby's tears. However, people do all kinds of things that they're not motivated to do in life, such as change dirty diapers, wash toilets, or get up and go to work. When they do, it's usually because the positive consequences of action are rewarding to them, or the negative outcomes of not doing it are painful.

Male Status at the Bargaining Table

Teresa Trull is a friend of mine who trains horses. She once observed that beginning women riders are sometimes so worried about hurting their horses that they get ignored by the animals. I see a parallel to this in my marriage therapy. Getting men to take on more is sometimes a matter of climbing on their backs, grabbing the reins, and spurring them in the direction you want them to go. If you're too timid in your assertions, they're more likely to keep munching the grass beneath their feet rather than lifting up their heads and trotting in the right direction. Of course, most men will fight a bridle, so don't go too far with my horse-riding metaphor.

Let's view it another way. I occasionally hear people display shock or incredulity when they meet a movie star who is friendly or unaffected. This always puzzles me. If anyone has cause to be friendly and approachable, it should be those who have the most going for them. However, this example is often played out in marriage with men playing the role of the movie star. Many are surprised when they hear that a husband does an equal amount of housework and parenting to his wife. This is because in the same way that the movie star doesn't have to be nice, most husbands don't have to do an equal amount of family work in order to pass muster.

I think the act of expressing gratitude and affection is always a good idea and should be at the center of every marriage. But let's be clear. Your husband's doing his fair share isn't a favor to you, it's an even exchange of services. Studies show that when men do favors, others feel that they should reciprocate more than when women do the same favors.[4] If you are to gain power in your household, you need to come face-to-face with the ways in which you may subtly or overtly idealize men or their power. You need to gain the comfort to face a man down and to strongly assert your wishes and needs for change. As Mahony writes, "Is there any way to expunge the glittery aura of male status? Only by changing one's feelings. Women who can't will scurry like a scullery maid or live with guilt."[5]

If you're reading this book, odds are that you're feeling taken advantage of, taken for granted, or simply doing more than is fair for you to do. In order to begin to reverse this situation, let's look at the various options that you have to get your partner to behave differently.[6] You can:

APPEAL TO HIS SENSE OF FAIR PLAY. This assumes that your partner has a sense of fair play and cares enough about you to be motivated by such a principle. If he does, that's an excellent place to start.

SUGGEST THAT CHANGING HIS BEHAVIOR WILL BENEFIT HIM IN SOME WAY. For example, if he does more, he'll get a happier wife in the process, something which he probably values and enjoys. It also benefits him because his taking on tasks may free you up to have energy to do some of the activities which he *does* value.

CASH IN ON A FAVOR. Remind him of what you've done for him and how he owes you one.

SHOW HIM HOW MUCH YOU'RE CONTRIBUTING. This can be done through lists, trading places for a day, or just telling him.

DISCLOSE HOW UNHAPPY YOU ARE WITH THE CURRENT ARRANGEMENT. Let him know, without whitewashing, how exhausted, resentful, or discouraged you are.

WORK WITH HIS PRIORITIES. Knowing your partner's priorities and pet peeves improves your bargaining position in marriage. Thus, if you are unsuccessful at eliciting your partner's support through discussions, you may have to outwait him on tasks that you know are a high priority for him. This will free up time and energy to devote to tasks which are a high priority to you.

CONSIDER ELIMINATING SOME OF THE CHORES. This means looking closely at what is really essential to your well-being and which activities you do out of habit or to please others.

MAKE TRADES. Let him know that you're willing to swap things or behaviors that he values for behaviors or items that you value.

IMPROVE YOUR BARGAINING POSITION. This can be done either through education, increasing your attractiveness, getting assertiveness training, getting counseling to help you understand your strengths and options, or decreasing your standards in regard to children and house.

So let's look at these options closely.

APPEAL TO HIS SENSE OF FAIR PLAY

Many men are aware of the disparity in the division of household labor and feel guilty about it.[7] Honest. I hear men in my practice talk about this, and the studies confirm it. I highlight this because I think many men do a good job of hiding that guilt because they don't know the best way to be involved and don't want their wives to use that guilt against them. Either way, let's *assume* that your husband feels guilty about how much more you do than him, even if his usual response is one of defensiveness or entitlement.

Let's take an example. Sandy and Mark have a four-month-old daughter. While Sandy worked full-time as an editor before their daughter was born, they have decided that because Mark makes more money, he will support them both. This gives Sandy an opportunity to be a full-time mom for the first few years of their daughter's life.

However, Sandy would like Mark to do more when he's home. She believes that while he supports the family financially, he has an eight-hour day, and she has a twenty-four-hour day. Mark promised to do a lot more before their daughter was born and Sandy's starting to get fed up with how little he's delivering.

So she should begin by appealing to his sense of fair play. Sandy should talk with Mark about the inherent lack of fairness in their arrangement. If Mark is a reasonable person and cares about her feelings, he may be motivated by her showing him that she has zero downtime in a twenty-four-hour period while he has considerably more than that. She should tell him specifically and concretely what he could do that would make her life easier when he's around. This conversation might go like this:

> **SANDY**: *I really appreciate how hard you work at your job and how you're supporting the family financially. It means a lot to me and I think it's great that we have the opportunity for me to be home full-time with the baby* [always lead with appreciation before a request]. *However, I'm wondering if you could help out a bit more when you're home. I know you're exhausted from your job,* [request, followed by empathy] *and I don't object to your spending some time on the computer or watching TV to unwind,* [empathy and understanding] *but after being up all night with the baby and being with her all day, I could use more help when you're home* [request].

Note that the request comes after stating her appreciation and her empathy for his perspective. If she didn't do that, he would more likely go into a counterproductive mode of defending himself.

SUGGEST THAT CHANGING HIS BEHAVIOR WILL BENEFIT HIM IN SOME WAY

Sandy should highlight that there is a win-win situation. She could say any of the following:

"I know you hate to see me so exhausted. If I got more rest, I'd have more energy to do some of the things you've been wanting to do on the weekends."

"It would be good for you and the baby to have some quality time together without me supervising it. You've said that you'd like that."

CASH IN ON A FAVOR

As with the principle of fairness, Sandy should make it clear that marriage and family life are a give and take. For example, every year Mark goes away on a fishing trip with his friends for a week. While this wasn't a burden prior to their daughter's birth, it *will* be burdensome now that she has a young child to look after. Therefore Sandy can emphasize that she's willing to have him go away again this year, but that she expects more in return. This conversation might go something like this:

SANDY: I know you have your fishing trip planned for the summer and we haven't really talked about whether that was going to keep happening once we had the baby [*introduces topic in nonargumentative, nonconflictual way*].

MARK: Why wouldn't it?

SANDY: I'm not saying that it wouldn't, only that we hadn't talked about it, and so I wanted to raise it with you. It will be a lot more work for me if I'm doing it as a single mother without your help [*here she ignores for the moment that he doesn't help that much anyway*].

MARK: So what are you saying?

SANDY: I'm saying that I'm willing to do it for you [*here I use the phrase "do it for you" to make it clear that this is now a* favor *that Sandy's doing for him rather than it being something he's entitled to, since they both agree, in principle, that everything shouldn't fall on her*]. However, I want you to do more to help when you're around. Here are some things you could do that would make me feel much better [*the request*].

Note also that Sandy says that his doing these activities will make her feel better. She doesn't use moralistic or shaming language, because that would trigger Mark's defensiveness and resistance.

SHOW HIM HOW MUCH YOU'RE CONTRIBUTING

Write out a list of what you do to contribute to the family. This will help you see what you're willing to trade off or negotiate. It can also help you feel more confident to demand more. Showing him the list may also affect his feelings of fair play and increase his participation. The conversation continues:

MARK: I'll only be gone for a week and all you have to do is take care of a baby all day. How hard is that? I think I deserve a week off with my friends given how hard I work.

SANDY: You do work hard and I do appreciate it [*empathy and appreciation; keeps it from escalating*]. However, taking care of a baby all day is hard work, too. In addition, my job doesn't end when I leave work. I do all of the laundry, all of the grocery shopping, I get up at night when the baby's hungry or needs to be changed, I balance the checkbook. We both work really hard and I don't begrudge you your trip. However, I expect you to do more so that everything doesn't always fall on me when we're both home [*lists her* *contributions in a matter-of-fact way and then ends with the request*].

Note

➤Let me emphasize that the most effective way to communicate her perspective is in a matter-of-fact, detached way rather than a victimized or burdened way. Her tone should be *affectionate though unmovable*. She should approach this situation as though she's made up her mind and that there's no way around it. However, she's confident that a successful option is there if they both look closely.

➤If this kind of coolheaded bargaining is foreign to you, it may be useful to practice with friends or use the assertiveness techniques in the exercises below. Again, women who get the most participation from men are those who are comfortably assertive in their expectations of that participation.[8] If you feel overly responsible or guilt-ridden about wanting your husband to pull his weight, you'll be at the mercy of his goodwill. This is *not* where you want to be in the modern-day, stressed-out marriage where everybody's trying to steal a few minutes of down time. If you're going to get more out of your husband, it will be because you've made it clear to him that something's gotta change, and you're not willing to keep running down this same rocky path.

DISCLOSE HOW UNHAPPY YOU ARE WITH THE CURRENT ARRANGEMENT

Some women have a hard time letting their partners know how unhappy they are because they believe they have no right to complain. This may be because:

- ➤ they grew up watching a mother take on too much responsibility
- ➤ their low self-esteem prevents them from feeling entitled
- ➤ their views of what women are supposed to do prevents them from demanding more

If any of these are true for you, it's critical that you work to feel more entitled. Unfortunately, some men are a little hard-of-hearing. This is why about a quarter of them are completely surprised when their wives file for divorce.[9] If you're talking to your husband about your feelings, you may have to make it very, very plain how unhappy you are with the current arrangement. In order for these conversations to be effective, they should look something like this:

SANDY: Our arrangement isn't working for me. Something has to change.

MARK: Why?

SANDY: I feel like I'm going to crack. It's too much. I can't get up with the baby three times a night, take care of her all day, do all of the laundry, all of the cleaning, all of the grocery shopping, fix you dinner, clean up after dinner, and then put the baby to bed by myself. It's too much.

MARK: But that's what we agreed on.

SANDY: I agreed to be a stay-at-home mom but neither of us had any idea about how hard it was going to be, and what a twenty-four-hour job it was. I'm starting to become miserable, and you don't want a miserable wife.

Note

➤ Again, Sandy's tone should be authoritative and immovable. It will probably take more than one of these conversations to get Mark onboard, and Sandy should be very concrete about what she expects him to do. It's not enough if she just says he should do more. *Don't let your guilt about wanting more out of your partner make you vague about what you want!* Guilt about asking for or demanding change is often at the heart of what motivates women to say, "He should just know!" Maybe he should, but you'll get more of what you want if you just tell him.

It's possible that if you felt less guilty about asking/demanding, you might not feel so annoyed. In fairness to your husband, he really may not know which activities are the most meaningful to you, and may need to be told, no matter how much you think he should know.

In this situation, Sandy needs to clearly spell out her needs. He'll benefit if she can move him in this direction because women's marital satisfaction goes way up when their husbands do almost *anything* to begin to lighten their workload. And men often do best if they know exactly what to do.

Bearing these principles in mind, Sandy should *create a to-do list* for Mark.

TO-DO LIST

➤ clean up after dinner (she might barter about how many times a week he should do it, but she should start her negotiation with *every night*)

➤ put the baby to sleep at least several nights a week

➤ give me a night or two off during the week to relax at home or go out with friends

➤ make dinner several nights a week

➤ take primary responsibility for the baby one of the two weekend days; if this is too hard to negotiate, at least one of the two weekend mornings so I can sleep in

➤ make the bed on the weekends

➤ spend more time with the baby when you're home

Note

➤ There's nothing magical about lists. They're only useful if they've been mutually agreed upon. If you haven't had the kind of conversation I'm suggesting and then thrust a list under your husband's nose, you'll either get ignored or resented. Men are overly sensitive to being told what to do. If they are persuaded to understand that they're making you happy by doing more, they'll be a lot more interested than if they're doing it because they're being told.

This interaction about the list will be less effective if Mark doesn't care how unhappy Sandy is. The more he cares about her and the more he can tune in to her feelings, the more he's likely to adjust his behavior. In general, the more affectionate

Sandy is with her tone of voice, the more likely that Mark will care about what she has to say. However, if he's not terribly committed to her or very sensitive, she'll have to play hardball, and go after what matters to him.

WORK WITH HIS PRIORITIES

If you are unsuccessful at eliciting your partner's support through straightforward discussions, you may have to outwait him on tasks that you know are a high priority for him. This will free up more time and energy to devote to tasks which are a high priority to you. Knowing your partner's priorities and pet peeves improves your bargaining position in marriage. For example, if Sandy currently pays the bills and Mark is someone who can't tolerate the bills being late, she could remove that task from her list because she knows that he won't let them accumulate.[10] This conversation might go like this:

SANDY: I don't have time to keep being in charge of paying the bills. Can you take it over?

MARK: I don't have time. You know how burned out I am when I come home from work. You have so much more free time than I do.

SANDY: Actually, I don't. It was fine before Shoshanna was born. But now I don't have a second to breathe. When she goes down for a nap, I'm doing laundry or cleaning up from breakfast or getting dinner ready. I don't have a second more.

MARK: Well, I really don't want to take it over.

SANDY: I completely understand but I just can't do it anymore.

And that should be the end of the discussion. If he persists, she should use what assertiveness trainers refer to as the broken-record technique.[11] This means that she keeps asserting, "I completely understand, but I just can't do it anymore because I'm doing too many other things," regardless of how he responds. The technique of outwaiting him on a task is only effective because she knows that Mark won't let the bills sit on the table unpaid. If she refuses to do them, he is forced to do them because it matters a lot to him. And so the "broken record" would play like this:

MARK: Seriously, Sandy, you've always done the bills.

SANDY: I completely understand but I just can't do it anymore because I'm doing too many other things.

MARK: That's not fair to me. I'm supporting the family, that's the least you can do.

SANDY: I'm doing a ton and I just can't do it anymore because I'm doing too many other things.

MARK: But you're better at managing that stuff than I am.

SANDY: I know, but I just can't do it anymore because I'm doing too many other things.

Sandy doesn't need to continue this conversation for very long. She should state it once or twice but stop paying the bills. This technique would not work with issues that Mark doesn't care about such as keeping the kitchen or the toilet clean. Therefore, if she were to say, "I refuse to keep cleaning the toilet" she'd be stuck with it since it matters more to her. This strategy only works with chores that you know he'll do if you don't.

CONSIDER ELIMINATING SOME OF THE CHORES

In most homes, something's gotta give. Sandy, for example, could consider eliminating some of the chores that she has taken on since the baby was born. While she should absolutely work to get Mark to do more, she may have to accept a somewhat higher degree of household clutter regardless of whether he jumps in to help or not.

HOW DO I LOWER MY STANDARDS?

Many women choose to accept some degree of exhaustion in order to maintain their standards of care for house and child.[12] It's a very personal decision, and only you can determine what's a healthy trade-off between standards of cleanliness and the amount of sacrifice required to achieve it. However, lowering your standards may be an important way to decrease your stress and increase your partner's willingness to do more.[13] This is because your standards of housework and parenting may be so high in comparison to your partner's that he has thrown up his hands and walked away from the bargaining table.

In other words, you can't completely accuse your husband of laziness if your standards are so high that he can never meet them. And the fact that your standards are high doesn't mean that they're necessarily right or the best for both of you. I have witnessed many a marriage get waylaid because the person with high standards believed that their ideals entitled them to belittle the other person's comparatively lower ones. Fights about standards can also be around organization, adventurousness, athletic ability, debates about whether to spend or save, sexual performance, whatever. This isn't to say that you should put up with the neglect of your children, or that you should live in squalor. It's just that most of the time, household chores can be done less frequently, and children can be attended to in a less-than-perfect fashion, and still thrive.

So let's consider what you could eliminate or reduce around the house or with the kids in order to get your husband to do more and free up more time for yourself. Here are some examples from other moms:

➤ SIMPLIFY MEALS. I have heard many mothers complain that they feel guilty if they don't spend a lot of time preparing their children's food. However, half the time, children don't even eat what's placed in front of them. I have not infrequently witnessed my own children push aside some nicely prepared (and pleadingly requested) meal only to go and get a string cheese out of the fridge. Children do need nutritious meals, but they really don't care if you spend a lot of time preparing them. The less time you spend cooking, the more time you have to do other things that are more pleasurable to you and maybe also to your family.

➤ CLEAN THE HOUSE LESS FREQUENTLY AND LESS THOR-OUGHLY. This may mean that the children wear the same jeans to school several days before they go in the laundry, towels don't get cleaned quite as often, or floors vacuumed as much. The world won't end, and your house won't be overtaken with vermin, no matter what your mother told you.

➤ DON'T BATHE THE KIDS EVERY SINGLE DAY. Okay, while they're in diapers they probably need some kind of a regular cleaning. However, as they get older, reducing the frequency of baths can free up time as well. The Europeans have been doing this for years and they don't appear to be any more disease prone than their cleaner American counterparts.

➤ **GET THE KIDS TO DO MORE**. Many parents don't have their kids do enough around the house. This may be because so many children are so overscheduled that their mothers don't want to add anything more to their already burdened little lives. However, consider the fact that it may burden them more to see their mothers exhausted and overwhelmed. In addition, having regular responsibilities around the house is useful for children's developing sense of self-esteem, and feelings of accomplishment.

Up to a certain age, most children view household chores as a pleasurable way to take on challenges or play grown-up. While toddlers can help a little, some parents don't involve them because supervising children adds to parental time rather than decreases it. However, while this process requires an initial investment, more time can be freed up for you as they become competent and take on more responsibility.

BELOW ARE SOME GUIDELINES FOR ACTIVITIES
WHERE CHILDREN CAN HELP

Clearing the dishes from dinner: *age four on;* earlier if using nonbreakable materials like plastic bowls, cups, and bottles
Putting away their toys and games: *toddler*
Making their bed: *age five on*
Cleaning their room: *toddlers can help with this task though children can't be expected to successfully clean a room until somewhat older.* They can do certain assigned tasks such as putting toys in a toy chest, dirty clothes in a hamper, etc.

Cooking: with supervision, *from age seven on*
Laundry: *early teens*
Mowing lawn: *teens*
Running errands: *teens*

MAKE TRADES

If Sandy wants Mark to do more, she should consider making a trade with him. However, she should be careful to exchange things of equal value. On the other hand, the more desperately she wants him to do something, the greater the trade-off she'll have to make.

Consider items or behaviors that are of value to your husband that are sometimes hard for you to give him:

- time alone
- weekend or nights out with his friends
- purchases (these should be of equivalent value to what you're requesting)
- doing things with him that he especially likes, which you don't (e.g., sporting events, certain types of movies, etc.)
- sleeping late on the weekends
- time with his children from prior marriage
- agreeing to spend time with the friends or family members of his that you're not so crazy about

IMPROVE YOUR BARGAINING POSITION

It may be that Sandy doesn't have enough power in her marriage to get Mark to be a better partner. If that's the case, she may need to develop long- and short-term strategies to improve her bargaining position. At present, Mark is holding his financial power over her head as a reason for doing a lot less than she. Over time, she may need to increase her financial power in the marriage by going back to work. If he is less committed to the marriage, she may also want to do other things that would improve her bargaining position such as increasing her attractiveness in the marital marketplace—not because she wants to divorce him but to let both of them know of her value and the potential dangers of ignoring her wishes.

For example, Victoria is a mother of twin five-year-old girls. While her husband promised to contribute equally to parenting and housework before children, he refused to do much of either after they arrived. Victoria applied many of the above suggestions, however they had little effect. Over time, her husband's refusal to do anything created huge feelings of resentment and desperation in her, and she began to frequently think about divorce. I encouraged her to let him know that she was entering the point of no return, and she did, but he continued to ignore her.

However, during this time, Victoria went back to the gym, lost twenty pounds, got buff, and finished her degree in nursing. Not surprisingly, Leon suddenly began to take her threats seriously and do more around the house. In other words, the fact that Victoria was now in a better position to be financially stable without his help and in a better position to attract another mate forced Leon to more closely consider what his life would be like without her.

Divorce Culture and Bargaining Power

In the past thirty to forty years, our culture has fundamentally changed in the ways that we think about marriage and divorce. Divorce, once considered a measure of last resort, is now an everyday occurrence. The freedom to divorce has increased women's power in marriage because they no longer have to remain in those that they find intolerable. This gives them the power to tell their husbands that if they don't change, they can leave.[14]

However, the consequences of divorce for women are still more dire than they are for men overall. Women are often punished when they divorce because they haven't accrued the kind of social security benefits or savings as their husbands. Less than a third of all women in the workforce participate in a private pension plan, and a scant 1 percent of part-time female workers have one.[15] Ann Crittenden observes that because women earn less over the course of their lifetimes, and typically have lower savings than men, a "geriatric gender gap" exists between the sexes. For example, in 1997, 14.7 percent of women over the age of sixty-five were poor, compared with only 8.2 percent of men.[16] She writes, "Because unpaid child care is not measured and counted as labor, caregivers earn zero social security credits for raising children at home. As a result, millions of American women forfeit billions of dollars a year in retirement income."[17]

These financial realities directly affect mothers' abilities to negotiate in marriage because their options, should they divorce, are far more dire than they are for fathers who have enjoyed uninterrupted funding of pensions and social security savings. In addition, men's careers are more solidly on track than those of career women who take a lengthy hiatus from their jobs to raise their children. Thus while men's earning potential has steadily climbed over time, women's earning potential typically decreases if they don't go back to work right away.

A woman is also more compromised in the case of divorce because 90 percent of the time, mothers, not fathers, become custodial parents.[18] This reality compromises women's bargaining position because it means that a divorce may make her life far more stressful than it already is. In other words, knowing that you could leave and do just fine may make you push a little harder and with more conviction for change than if you believe, rightly or wrongly, that you need your partner's income, assistance, or companionship to survive. While you and your partner may never divorce, your ever-changing standing in the marriage market affects both of your perspectives about your bargaining power.

Let's look at this in more detail. Cathy is an attractive obstetrician and the mother of a two-year-old girl. She has become deeply resentful of the fact that her husband, a professor, does little or nothing around the house, and is uninvolved as a dad. She has recently decided that she wants to discuss the unfair division of labor at home between her and her husband. Cathy knows that if she can't find a way to motivate her partner, and eventually decides to divorce, her chances are good that she can remarry. This is because she is financially in a good position to support herself and her child. In addition, her youth and beauty make her desirable in the marriage market. This is not to say that Cathy would or should threaten to divorce her husband, nor that the effects of the divorce on her or her daughter would be benign. Rather, divorce is a card that she can play if she has to. From a pure bargaining standpoint, Cathy's position is good.

Let's contrast her bargaining power with that of Jessica, a full-time mother with a high school education and a two-year-old daughter. While Jessica is the same age as Cathy, and equally attractive, she has far less bargaining power in her negotiations with her husband because of her financial dependence on him. Her youth and beauty increase her odds of finding a good partner if she divorces, but her financial dependence makes the prospect of divorce a riskier venture. This knowledge could make Jessica a little more docile in her negotiations, and her husband a little more comfortable ignoring her requests for change.

In comparing these two women, it's clear that Cathy the obstetrician has much more power with which to get her husband to change than does Jessica. If Cathy needs to give her husband an ultimatum, he will have more cause to take her seriously. He knows that she's an attractive woman and that she isn't dependent on him to make her way in the world if they split up.

Jessica's husband has more power to ignore her threats. While he knows that she's attractive enough to interest another man, he also knows that she would have to pay a high price for living without his ongoing financial support as a part- or full-time mother. These realities, even if left unstated by everybody, factor into the subtle, ongoing, day-to-day negotiations that occur in every home.

The Husband's Power (or Lack Thereof)

Both wives' bargaining positions are relative to the husband's other forms of power in the marriage. Cathy the obstetrician is married to a man who earns far less than does she. In this situation, Cathy's power is increased even more greatly in the marriage because her husband is more likely to suffer financially if they divorce. Not surprisingly, studies show that in those homes where the wife earns more than the husband, he typically does more parenting and housework.[19]

However, men who earn more don't always feel or behave more powerfully in marriage. Their financial power is no guarantee of greater influence at home if they are more committed to the marriage than their wives, or if they're less able to be assertive. In other words, it isn't solely an issue of finances, it's also a function of who is more invested in the marriage.

Some version of this exists for Jessica. Jesssica and her husband met in high school. While he has changed little over the course of their marriage, she has grown and blossomed. Even though Jessica's husband has more financial power than she, he would be far more affected by a divorce because of his attachment to her. This reality serves to increase Jessica's bargaining position in the marriage, and offsets her lower degree of relative financial power.

While housework is a conflict for many couples before children arrive, it ain't nothin' compared to what it's like after the kids come. In the next chapter we'll look at the ways in which children have affected your feelings about your partner, yourself, and your marriage, and what may need to change in order for you to gain a more fair division of labor in your household.

Once Children Arrive

Here's a little-known fact: When a couple has children, their marriage typically takes a turn for the worse and doesn't fully recover till the wee ones trot off to college.[1] Little wonder. Despite expectations, a new child means a huge shift of attention and resources away from our "selves" into the nonnegotiable well-being of this new, little, darling, impossible, crying, fantastic human. And what most couples learn is that gaining the identity of *husband* or *wife* is nothing compared to the many meanings and implications of gaining the identity of *mother* or *father*.

Because not only do we have to make a fundamental shift in how we see ourselves, we have to shift in the way we see our spouses too. *My husband* is now *the father of my children*. *My wife* is now *my children's mom*. While each addition of roles carries an opportunity for growth, depth, and meaning, it also carries the potential for stress, conflict, and misunderstanding.

Becoming a parent also means revisiting what it was like when we were children, and this, too, can be an area of both pleasure and stress. On the positive side, it's an opportunity to recall or relive pleasant childhood memories or feelings. On the stressful side, it's an opportunity to relive painful childhood memories and feelings.

> RHONDA: *Being a parent has made me remember a lot of what my childhood was like. In some ways, it's made me a little more sympathetic to how impatient my parents were. On the other hand, there's no way I'm going to raise my children the way that they raised me.*

Many parents discover that becoming a parent is one of the few opportunities life offers to heal the hurts or disappointments that occurred in their own childhood. In being a better parent than theirs were, they are able to give their children what they never received. While becoming a parent truly *is* an important opportunity for personal growth, some parents, moms in particular, make the mistake of pushing the marriage to the back burner and ironically create the very dynamic they sought to avoid. At the same time, many fathers shift from being decent, sensitive husbands to dumping all of the new household and parental chores on their already burdened and bewildered wives.

This chapter will look at the effect that children have had on your marriage, and on you and your partner. We'll look at how the stresses of parenthood may be interfering with getting your husband to participate more equitably, and what may need to change in order to go forward.

Becoming a Team

University of California at Berkeley psychologists Carolyn and Philip Cowan found that the three most important predictors of couples who successfully made the transition to becoming parents were:

1. having a clear sense of who they were
2. being able to stand back far enough from a marital conflict to see and understand the other's perspective
3. neither avoiding conflicts nor prolonging them.[2]

In general, men who have a good sense of who they are and who don't feel burdened by a woman's needs are better able to make the transition to becoming parents than those who don't. This is because they are able to be both reassuring and helpful at the same time. They can comfortably make that all-important shift from a more "me-centered" identity to one that is "we-centered."

While becoming a new mother doesn't always produce a greater dependency, it certainly produces a greater need for an *inter*dependence between a husband and wife. Unfortunately, some men have an allergic reaction to almost *any* form of dependency on the part of their wives. Men whose own mothers were overly demanding, needy, or restrictive can feel especially frightened by their wife's sudden escalation in needs and requirements for help. A woman may be suddenly caught off guard by this new demonstration of anger, withdrawal, or blame in response to her reasonable requests for help and participation.

ADRIANA: *Tim used to be a pretty low-key guy before the baby. I don't think he hardly ever got mad. Since then, I've seen a totally different side of him and it isn't for the better. He makes me feel like I'm completely inconveniencing him if I make one request. I constantly feel like I'm this totally needy thing that he has to get away from.*

TIM: *Adriana and I had a pretty good marriage before kids, but I had no idea what it was going to be like. All of a sudden it's "Can you help me with this? Can you do that?" I just feel like, "Damn, you're the mom. Why do you expect me to do so much?"*

Men who have unresolved issues with their own parents may respond to their wives' needs for increased help by withdrawing into hobbies, work, or a host of other activities that keep them at a distance from her worry, exhaustion, and anxiety.[3] This produces a common negative feedback loop where:

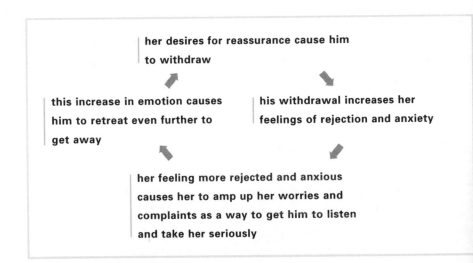

her desires for reassurance cause him to withdraw

his withdrawal increases her feelings of rejection and anxiety

her feeling more rejected and anxious causes her to amp up her worries and complaints as a way to get him to listen and take her seriously

this increase in emotion causes him to retreat even further to get away

And on and on, all the way to the next round of alienation or fighting.

Moving to "We"

A sense of we-ness is best achieved if *both* spouses are doing their part to reach out to the other. Unfortunately, many men feel rejected by their wives' preoccupation with the baby and her relative lack of preoccupation with him. In many ways, men feel that the "we" they once knew as a couple has been replaced by the "we" of mother to child.

Most men feel better about their marriages when their wives are able to manage the stress and anxiety of being a new mother and demonstrate some degree of independence around it.[4] Mothers who let their worries about the baby crowd out the marriage often make their husbands feel burdened and resentful.

> IRA: *Millie has always been a worrier but I could manage it before the baby was born. Since then, Jesus, it's a nonstop anxiety show. I bet I get seven calls a day about some worry she has. "The baby hasn't eaten much this morning, the baby has a rash on its arm, the baby this, the baby that." Sometimes I feel like just saying, "Can't you just deal with it?" It's incredibly aggravating.*

Women's Identity

While dad's stress level rises for the first month of a child's life, a mothers' stress level continues to rise over the first *year*.[5] A large part of this difference stems from the physical and hormonal changes mothers experience from carrying a baby for nine months, nursing it, and getting up in the middle of the night to care for it. In addition, a woman who was a good sleeper before having children may permanently lose that capacity once she becomes a mother.[6]

Women's identities may also be affected by how their bodies change as a result of pregnancy. In one study, "loss of figure" and "general unhappiness about appearance" topped the lists of most of the women's complaints about being new mothers.[7]

> **THERESA**: *I put on a lot of weight with my twins and I still haven't been able to get it off, even though they're one-year-olds now. Ron says my weight doesn't bother him, but I know it does because we hardly ever have sex anymore. I can't stand feeling fat, but with these kids it's been impossible to find any time to exercise.*

A new mother's increase in exhaustion and decreased security about her attractiveness can translate into a greater need for reassurance and care from her husband. Since a new father typically has far more time and energy than a new mother, his wife's inability to live up to his expectations isn't a crisis. However, when a husband doesn't live up to his wife's expectations for help, it *is* a crisis because she has far fewer stores of sleep or energy from which to draw.[8]

LINDA: *Since my kids have been born I feel like I'm on the verge of a nervous breakdown. It's just so much work and I feel like Ron expects me to do everything! It's really unfair.*

Some children are harder to parent, and this can make a mother depressed or anxious, no matter how her identity is created, or how much her husband is helping.[9] Children who are disabled, colicky, have attentional problems, learning disabilities, or psychiatric diagnoses can cause parents to feel ashamed, afraid, resentful, and overwhelmed. If your child has any of these, it's very important that you get adequate support and time for yourself. Feeling alone with difficult children can cause depression and anxiety.

For all of these reasons, mothering may be a far more stressful process than fathering. As children get older, many mothers find that children continue to pull more on them for emotional support and reassurance than from father. While this can be a source of pleasure, it's also a huge responsibility that can be both stressful and draining.

However, many men have a hard time understanding why women are so stressed by parenting.

RANDY: *Dina always complains about how whiny and demanding the kids are but I never have that problem when I have them. They almost never cry when it's just me and them. I think it's because she gives in too much to them.*

Men's confusion over this issue likely stems from the fact that children depend on their mothers in a way that's more draining and demanding. In the same way that our children may be well behaved at school and then break down when they get home, they seem the most likely to be their whiniest, neediest, and most difficult when mom's around. Why? Fundamentally, they may not *have* to be as well behaved around her because they're used to her being more attentive when she's with them. Dad's care, in most homes, is less available and consistent. Also, the behavior of crying, whining, or begging may be more likely to pull on a mother's heartstrings and call her to action far more than it does for fathers.[10]

Women who have a good resource of supports and outside interests tend to do better than those who don't. For example, those who think of themselves as mothers but also gain their identity through work, friendships, and marriage are more resilient and less vulnerable to depression than those who gain most of their identity from being a mom.[11] This is partly because parenting is unpredictable in its rewards. Children, especially infants, can be difficult and not all that much fun to hang out with. Women who believe that being a mother should determine their identities are more likely to feel guilt and anxiety if they find the job ungratifying. In addition, as we saw in the last chapter, women who are full-time mothers may be more dependent financially on their husbands, and have less leverage to negotiate for the changes in their marriages or lives that would make them feel happier. They can feel more dumped on by their husbands with fewer recourses to fight back.

The Crisis of Children

However, the arrival of children is a crisis point in any marriage because both the husband and wife suddenly have to draw on abilities and resources that may never have been developed before. Children commonly create feelings of deprivation in sleep, time for ourselves, time with our partners, and worry about money. These stresses make it far more likely that couples are going to fight.

ARIANNA: *Billy and I hardly ever fought before the kids and now that's all we do. I almost can't tell that we're the same people.*

It's not surprising that there's an increase in conflict given the amount of work that's created with the arrival of a child. For example, infants typically need to be diapered six or seven times a day, soothed two to three times a night and as many as five times a day. Laundry increases from one or two loads a week to four or five, dishwashing from once a day to four times a day, grocery shopping from one trip a week to three, house-cleaning from once weekly to once a day. It's a huge increase of work in a very, very short time.[12]

Unfortunately, in most homes, the burden of this increase in work gets absorbed by the mother. For example, a baby who is breast-fed and not given bottles will spend between four to six hours a day nursing.[13] This not only gives mom more opportunity to attach to her newborn, it increases the opportunity and likelihood that the baby will become more attached to her. As any pet owner knows, the person who provides the food gains a special place in the recipient's heart, and infants are not immune to this key to survival. In addition, many mothers feel deeply gratified by the unique place that they have in their baby's life and aren't always eager to dilute it by sharing the glory with their often willing husbands.

However, this unique bond that mother and newborn feel

for each other automatically stacks the deck toward mom doing more, especially if dad is not very active between feedings.[14] Baby soon learns to associate comfort with mother, a fact that often continues well into adulthood. The classic example I hear in my practice and in letters from mothers has to do with a wish that their husbands would intervene in the care of the baby far more frequently, and far more quickly. While there may be different standards of care, many dads don't get up off the floor, couch, bed, lawn chair, divan, or sofa as often or as rapidly because they knows that their wives will. In an environment of limited resources of time and energy, these sometimes subtle differences become big sources of tension when played out day after day. One researcher found that when women work full-time outside the home, her contributions to care for house and child still exceeded her husband's contributions by a much as 300 percent.[15]

One counterbalance to this syndrome is what Mahony terms "affirmative action for fathers." By this she means that the amount of time that the mother spends nursing should be offset with an equal amount of time with dad.[16] This is a challenge for many mothers because it means that they have to tolerate her baby's discomfort as it learns to accept nurturance from the dad. It is a particularly important point in a relationship, however, because those moms who don't do it will end up with a lot more work.

What Do Others Think of Me?

Becoming a mother creates a whole new set of opportunities for social rewards and censure. Because women's identities have been traditionally more oriented around children and house, new mothers may feel especially vulnerable to others' judgments in these two areas. Gaining control over your fear of others' judgments is critical to your finding a way to relax your standards enough to get your husband involved and free up more time for yourself.

> **PAULA**: *I used to freak out whenever someone would just drop by and I hadn't had time to do a thorough housecleaning. I'd go crazy if there were cups in the sink or one of the boys' shirts was hanging over the couch. "Oh, they're going to think I'm such a slob." After a while I decided that my mental health depended on not being so worried about what they thought.*

Women who were raised by stay-at-home mothers often feel conflicted by living a life at odds with how their mothers lived. Some feel subtly or overtly criticized for working outside of the home, or for having lower standards of care for the house.[17]

> **LIANNE**: *My mother makes me feel terrible about working, and I have to work because we need the money. She's constantly saying things like, "Don't you think it's bad for the kids for you to be gone so much? Do you have to work so many hours?" It's not like when she was growing up, where my dad put all of us through college on a dockworker's salary.*

Now you need both parents working full-time to even be barely middle class. Besides, I'd go crazy being a full-time mom and she just doesn't get that.

Compared to Mom

For better or worse, we all compare ourselves to our parents. This is another area where men have an easier row to hoe. It doesn't take a lot of effort for us men to be better parents or housekeepers than our dads, because most of our fathers weren't that involved in either arena. Women don't have this easy comparison because they were raised by mothers who, on average, didn't work outside the home, and were available to them full-time. While many working women feel a sense of pride from taking advantage of the opportunities that their mothers have never experienced, they often feel guilty about not being as available to their children.[18] This may make them vulnerable to accusations from parents, friends, society, and in-laws.

> PENNY: *Whenever my mother-in-law comes over I can feel the judgment. She's like the mother-in-law from some sitcom where she's always making these digs about feeling sorry for me that I can't keep up with the house or keep the kids clean. I always dread it when she's going to stop by because I feel like I have to rush around and make the house neat and make sure the boys don't have any peanut butter on their faces or that they haven't left their Gameboys strung out across the living room.*

This is a common scenario with in-laws, and therefore worth reviewing in some detail. In this scenario, Penny has three options:

1. ignore her mother-in-law's comments
2. get her husband to get his mother off Penny's back
3. confront her mother-in-law

Let's look at the first option. In order to ignore her mother-in-law's criticism, Penny would have to *get control over her belief that she should care about what her mother-in-law thinks*. She should begin by exploring why her mother-in-law's opinion matters so much to her. Is it because her husband is also judgmental of her in these arenas and she's worried that he'll ally with his mom against her? Are her own parents critical of her, and this makes her more inclined to believe others when they are critical? Does she compare herself to her mother's standards of parenting and cleanliness and now believes that anything short of that is an indictment?

Regardless of the cause, Penny *must decide whether it's worth it to work so hard to fend off other's judgments*. She would be wise to strongly consider this option. The advantage of learning to care less about what others think is that it would:

1. free up more time for her to do activities that are more rewarding
2. increase the likelihood that her husband will participate more because she'll have to become more assertive and more flexible in her standards
3. help her to strengthen herself against others' judgments of her in the rest of her life

Penny's other option is to *get her husband involved in telling his mother to back off*. Marital researcher John Gottman found that couples who prioritize their marriage over their in-laws have better marriages than those who allow the in-laws too much influence.[19] It's especially important to a couple's well-being and longevity if the *husband* has sufficiently separated from his parents and is able to prioritize his wife's happiness over his own mother's.[20] Men who are too tied to their own parents may give their parents too much say over how to conduct their households.

If Penny's husband hasn't stood up to his mother regarding her hurtful and intrusive comments, Penny should begin by telling him that she'd like him to start making supportive comments about Penny whenever mommy-in-law gives one of her not-so-subtle criticisms. Some examples of supportive comments are:

> *"Yes, it's amazing how much Penny gets done in a day. I've never met anyone like her."*
> *"Yeah, it's harder on mothers these days than it used to be. They have much more responsibility."*

If these more subtle strategies don't work, he should switch to something more pointed such as "Mom, that sounds like a dig. Penny works extremely hard." He should keep it up until mom gets the point, though it may be better for him to speak to her when Penny isn't around. The key part of the interaction is getting her husband to prioritize his marriage over his relationship with his mother.

This will take some influence and action on Penny's part. She should engage this by:

➤ reminding him that it's his mother and therefore his responsibility to get her to behave
➤ telling him that he'll have a happier wife if he does, and a potentially resentful one if he doesn't

➤ letting him know that she's not the one putting him into a loyalty battle, his mother is

➤ reminding him that, if push comes to shove, Penny has a right to ask him to prioritize her happiness over his mother's

➤ telling him that she will talk to the mother if he won't, but that won't strengthen the marriage and may hurt it

➤ if he agrees to talk to his mother, Penny will feel closer to him as long as he doesn't blame Penny if it goes poorly

If none of those work, Penny should begin to confront her mother-in-law herself. Again, she should begin with subtle, friendly reproaches and if those don't work, go to something more direct. Examples of a more direct approach are:

"It makes me feel bad when you say that to me. I'm sure you don't mean to. But it makes me feel like you think I'm a bad mother and wife."

Or, more pointedly,

"I don't like the way you talk to me about my parenting and housecleaning. I need you to stop."

Again, whether it's being initiated by your husband or you, to your in-law or to a parent, it should go in stepwise fashion from pleasant and subtle to direct and overt. Ideally, your husband would take responsibility because it's better for your marriage if he sets the boundaries with his parents than you. On the other hand, if he won't, and your in-laws' comments continue to make you feel bad, then you'll have to take the lead.

The Identity Shift for Men

W hile a father's life becomes more stressful after a newborn, his stress levels off after the first month. In addition, most men describe the arrival of children as deeply meaningful, however it's less common for them to experience a profound change in their identity in the way that many mothers do.[21] Overall, fathers are more likely to want to resume their prior schedule of involvement with friends, hobbies, and work after the arrival of the first child. This is probably because they are less tethered to the baby by nursing, don't have to recover from childbirth, and aren't burdened with hormonal changes. In addition, dads generally go through a smaller amount of change in how they think of themselves. This is because men's identity traditionally has been more around work than family. However, it's not uncommon for the arrival of children to cause men to experience increased anxiety about intrusive in-laws and finances.[22]

> **KEN**: *I wasn't that worried about money before Sara was born. Somehow, we always found a way to make ends meet. But since she's been born I worry a lot about it. All of a sudden I'm thinking college, braces, car insurance, yikes. I'm freaking out about it.*

While many men seek to be better fathers (and sometimes, housekeepers) than theirs were, most lack the inner compass or image to determine what constitutes a fair share. Like you, he may be compromised by being too sleep-deprived, overwhelmed, and worried about money to know the best way to share the workload after children. While I often hear mothers say in regard to their husbands, "He should just know," they often don't.

A Lower Sex Drive

One of the biggest sources of male marital satisfaction is sexual frequency.[23] Unfortunately, during the first year after a child is born, sexual frequency drops in 30 to 40 percent of couples because the wife loses interest due to stress, exhaustion, and hormonal changes.[24] This causes some men to pull back from their wives, feeling rejected or angry. Tragically this occurs at a time when their wives need them the most. Couples appear to make the transition through the trials of a new baby when the husband is able to prioritize his wife's increased need for emotional support and physical involvement, and where she is able to balance her love affair with the baby with her husband's needs for attention, affection, and acknowledgment.[25]

NEAL: *I understand that Ida is stressed by the baby but I'm really not into being celibate. If we make love on a regular basis, I feel really close to her, and frankly, a lot more willing to do whatever it is she wants me to do. If we go months without it, like we have been, I just start feeling like she's some roommate or something and she starts getting seriously on my nerves.*

While a mother's fascination, love for, or worry about her offspring can cause her to think and talk about little else, men can feel both bored and rejected if their wives have no other conversational focus.[26] Again, this may have to do with how central a baby becomes in a mother's life. For example, a survey found that 17 percent of new mothers described the baby's first step as a "big thrill" while only 1 percent of new fathers did.[27] In addition, if mothers are spending more time around their children than fathers, as a majority do, it makes sense that their conversational focus would be more child centered. However, it's also understandable that a father may be less interested if he's spending less time and is also involved in other activities.

As a way to determine how your marriage has changed since children, consider the following questions:

Since we've become parents:
I've become more impatient
I'm more irritable
I'm more depressed
I worry more
I need my husband more
I am less interested in my husband than ever
I feel lonely
I gained more weight
I feel less interested in sex
I'm happier
my life is more meaningful

In what ways has your husband changed? He's become:
more self-centered
less sympathetic
less available

more withdrawn

more irritable

happier

more responsible

In what ways have the two of you changed as a couple since children? We:

fight more

spend less time together

have less sex

worry more about money

feel closer

Note

➤ Many men show love through *doing* rather than *saying* (such as talking about feelings or providing emotional support). Women who are able to accept this difference and appreciate the ways their husbands contribute are more likely to have better marriages.[28] Often, marital satisfaction rises or falls on the basis of how much or how little the members show appreciation for what the other contributes. This is tied to what Hochschild refers to as the "economy of gratitude."[29] Bearing this in mind, consider the following:

While you may be mad at your husband right now, what are the ways that he does contribute to the family?

income

yard or repair work

managing finances

planning vacations or time together

washing the cars

fixing or maintaining appliances, computers, etc.

spending time with the children (even if this is in ways that
you don't prefer such as watching TV or hanging out)

cooking

prioritizing time together away from the children such as
dates, etc.

**As an experiment, increase your appreciation for what he
does as a husband or father. At least once a day, simply
say, "Thanks for doing x or y, I really appreciate that."**

Assume That He Wants to Make You Happy

M ost husbands do want to make their wives happy—
they just get locked into power struggles, or they don't
know what works. Bearing that in mind, make concrete suggestions that are achievable. Have a long-term perspective and assume that it will require weekly to semiweekly monitoring or
discussing.

APPROACH WITH AFFECTION RATHER THAN AGGRESSION

Again, I'm not saying that attitude is everything—it isn't. But it's
a foundation that other behaviors such as bargaining can get or-
ganized around. If you're too aggressive, you'll get stonewalling
from your husband. Hetherington (2002) and others found that

the *pursuer-distancer* dynamic creates the most divorce-prone dynamic in a marriage.[30] In this scenario, one spouse, typically the wife, pursues the husband for more (fill in the blank: intimacy, conversation, housework, parenting, affection) while the other responds by withdrawing into silence and resentment. It's a cycle that both participate in driving downward. Clearly, if your husband woke up tomorrow and decided to do more, you wouldn't have to pursue him. Since that's not too likely, you'll want to see what needs to change in you to create the possibility of change in him. Again, if you came from a home where there was abuse, neglect, or divorce, there's a far greater likelihood that you need to work on your communication and conflict-management skills to create the changes you deserve.

Note

➤ In marriage, the lyrics are rarely as important as the melody. It isn't so much what we communicate but *how* we communicate it.

Commit to Change

In a moment of affection, tell him something you'd like him to make a commitment to change.

LANGUAGE FOR CHANGE

Pay attention to how you make requests. The following are recommended ways to communicate your requests:

Instead of ➤	Say ➤
You're always disappointing me.	I'd like you to do x or y.
You won't change.	Is there a way we can make sure it happens?
You don't care about me.	When you do things without my telling you, I feel really cared about.
You never do it.	Let's talk about how we can make sure that there's follow-through.

If he does something that you want him to do, reward the hell out of him for it. Try not to see this as a moral battle. The reality is probably that you're doing a lot more than he is and nobody's thanking *you* for it. However, one way to get him to change is to use positive reinforcement, just like Skinner with his pigeons. Not because it's your role in life but because it probably ain't gonna happen any other way.

I understand you may be too annoyed with him to lavish praise on him, and in all likelihood, what he does pales in comparison to what you contribute, or you wouldn't be spending your precious time reading *The Lazy Husband*, you'd be reading something a lot more fun. However, if the goal is to increase his involvement, we have to start somewhere.

If your husband were reading this book I'd encourage him

to do his part to make your marriage work—I've devoted Chapter 8 to that because I figure one chapter may be about as much as he'll be willing to read. However, since he's probably not reading alongside you, I have to focus on you, and make sure you're doing everything possible to hold up your end of the bargain. In addition to increasing your bargaining power and your communication, this also means monitoring your sex life, your levels of affection, and your acknowledgment of the ways he's contributing. Too often couples get stalemated, saying that they won't change until the other changes. However, this only buries a marriage in endless, unproductive waiting.

Foundations

What Kind of Marriage Do I Have?

Our beliefs about what men and women should do with the house and children are often central to what we end up doing—at least for women. Men are a little trickier. For example, while most young men currently believe that they should share housework equally, most don't.[1] This is an important finding because, among other things, it means that you're not crazy. Your husband may well believe in an equality between the sexes and, at the same time, act as though he doesn't!

In this chapter, we'll look at three different belief systems: traditional, egalitarian, and transitional (those that are in transition from traditional to egalitarian).[2] We'll look at marriages where the couples have different belief systems, and look at how conflict can be reduced and participation increased when ideas clash. Finally, we'll examine how your husband's and your beliefs contribute to the current dynamics in your marriage and determine what may have to change in order to make your family function more fairly.

The Traditional Marriage

Traditional couples commonly have the following characteristics:

Both believe that the woman should be the authority and caretaker of the house and children.

Both believe that the man should be the primary, if not the sole, breadwinner.

Both perceive that whatever parenting and housework the husband does is "helping his wife" rather than participating in an equal partnership.

The man may not be very involved as a parent.

Neither expects the woman to provide family income. When she does, she is expected to prioritize the children over her career.

Both believe that a father is no substitute for a mother.[3]

Transitional Marriage

A transitional marriage features a belief system somewhere between traditional and egalitarian. It has the following characteristics:

Both believe the wife has a right to a career.

While both believe the wife can and will provide family income, both think that she should prioritize the family over her career. This means that she will most likely be the one to make doctor's appointments, miss work, and oversee the household.

The man wants to be an active and involved father. He may wish to be the kind of father he never had.

Both believe that the woman should be the authority regarding parenting and household management.

Both probably perceive the husband's role in parenting and housework as "helping his wife" rather than seeing it as an equal partnership.

Both believe that a father is no substitute for a mother.[4]

Egalitarian Marriage

In an egalitarian marriage, both members believe that differences between the sexes are unimportant in regard to parenting, career, and housework. An egalitarian marriage has the following characteristics:

Both believe the woman has a right to a career.

Both believe the woman can and, in all likelihood, will provide family income (though some egalitarian couples choose to have the woman be a stay-at-home mother if they can afford it).

Neither husband nor wife assume that the wife is better able to parent the children, nor more obligated to make sacrifices on their behalf.

The man wants to be an active and involved parent. He may wish to be the kind of dad he never had. He assumes that

> his contributions as a parent are no less important than
> his wife's.
> Both believe that they are equally responsible to make doc-
> tor's appointments, miss work, oversee the household, etc.[5]

Let's look more closely at these couples through some examples.

A TRADITIONAL COUPLE:

·

Lynn and Robert

Lynn was raised in a small town in the Midwest. Her father was a factory worker and her mother a homemaker. She described her childhood as close and secure.

LYNN: *My mom was there every day when I got home from school and I really liked that. I know it sounds kinda corny to say that she was there with the baked cookies and all that, but she really was. She was very active in PTA and was really a supermom. My father was a good man, very quiet, but when he spoke, you knew he meant business. We lived in a small community where you went to grade school with the same kids you went to high school with, and everybody knew what everybody else was doing. I'm not saying it was perfect, but I really liked all of that, so I wanted to give my kids the same kind of childhood that I got.*

Lynn's marriage has a traditional division of labor. Her husband, Robert, is the sole breadwinner and decides how money will be spent in the family. He's good at fixing things around their house, and makes sure that their two cars run well and have regular servicing. While Robert spends more time with his children than his own father did with him, he defers to Lynn around most parenting matters. In addition, he spends far less of his free time engaged with the children or the house than does Lynn.

Like her mother, Lynn is good at cooking and running a household. She takes pride in her ability to make their home comfortable and attractive while living within a strict budget. She is an active and involved mother, capable of juggling the many competing school and athletic interests of her kids.

Economist Rhona Mahony observes that specialized roles create advantages for a couple that may not occur in homes where the roles are less clear.[6] In *Kidding Ourselves: Breadwinning, Babies, and Bargaining Power,* she writes, "High levels of performance in unpaid family work can create a special, warm atmosphere at home. Couples in which both parents work for pay full-time at demanding jobs cannot bring off many of those extra domestic touches. They may pay that price willingly. Still they pay it." The other advantage that occurs with clear roles is that there is less room for misinterpretation over who does what. This is one of the reasons why traditional couples have fewer conflicts over housework and parenting.[7]

One of the biggest stresses that traditional women face is the exhaustion from being a full-time homemaker.[8] As a result, they often expect their husbands to do at least *something* around the house. However, the amount of family work that traditional men do is often a balance between how assertive the wife is and how sensitive the husband is. Hochschild found that some women get traditional men to do more by feigning incompetence or illness.[9] This may work because it dramatizes the importance of the task to the man, or because it provides him a way of feeling strong while doing something outside of his comfort zone. Part of the reason that men do more when women request help of their traditional husbands (as opposed to demand it) is that it gets them around the idea that they're doing something contrary to their views of themselves as men. In the same way that some men reassure themselves that their wives are employed because they "allow it," men can claim that they're "helping" their wives with family work to maintain a feeling that it's not a big part of who they are.[10]

While traditional women may want their husbands to help, traditional men who are less sensitive to a wife's needs for help with the house and kids typically won't produce as much resentment in his wife than it would in a transitional or egalitarian wife. This is because a transitional or egalitarian wife will experience the husband's lack of participation as a betrayal of shared values and beliefs. A traditional wife assumes that if push comes to shove, the house and kids fall on her side of the family work line.[11]

THE DOWNSIDE OF TRADITIONAL MARRIAGE

While there are advantages to women who choose the traditional arrangement, there are also disadvantages to women. Women in traditional marriages typically have less bargaining power than women in marriages who bring in income and social status.[12] This is because the former group are more likely to be financially dependent on their husbands and more economically vulnerable in the case of a divorce. They are also more likely to believe that a wife should defer to a husband's authority. This combination often weakens their ability to renegotiate the marital rules or to challenge its terms. In addition, a traditional woman may not have developed some of the hard-boiled negotiating skills that people learn through the competitive environment of the work-place.[13] All of these serve to make her position in the marriage somewhat more contingent on the benevolence of her husband.

Many women resent being in the position of having to ask for help because it feels like begging for something they feel entitled to have.[14] As a result, some manage their resentment by deceiving themselves into thinking that they're more accepting of the household arrangement than they really are. They tell themselves that it's okay because their husbands are incompetent, they won't do it right, or they shouldn't have to do as much because it doesn't matter to them as much.

A TRANSITIONAL COUPLE:
•
Jolene and Ivan

A transitional couple believes that the husband should do more with the house and kids than a traditional one, however the wife should have more say than the husband. Both believe that the wife has a right to a career and, often, an expectation that she'll contribute money to the family. While couples with this belief system share similar ideas, putting those concepts into practice are often harder than they are for couples at either end of the spectrum.[15] This is because both sexes may be ambivalent or confused about what's expected of them. A woman who believes that her husband should be a very involved father may feel guilty about sharing her child or relinquishing her control over household duties. A man who believes that his wife has a right to her own time may feel more ambivalent when he has to sacrifice his time to provide for it. She may end up gate-keeping, and he may end up doing a lot of dumping and deferring rather than taking the lead with parenting or housecleaning.

This was true of Jolene and Ivan. Jolene loved that Ivan wanted to be a committed father but had a hard time letting him be one. She cringed whenever he picked up their baby son and constantly gave him "ideas" of how he should take care of him. From her perspective, she spent much more time with their son, so it was only logical that she would better know how he should be handled. This viewpoint extended to the housework as well.

Ivan wasn't a slob but he wasn't meticulous either. Once their son was born he was overwhelmed with how much work there was to do. While he had intended to "help out" a lot prior to the baby's birth, his exhaustion and his belief system caused him to push the majority of the work onto Jolene. Not surprisingly, they ended up frequently fighting about who was going to do what with the house and kids.

As sociologist and family researcher Jay Belsky writes, "We estimated that even if a couple only bumps heads three or four times a day about diapering, the day-care pickup, or responsibility for the night shift, by the end of the first year they will have received between 1,000 and 1,500 reminders that in their marriage there are two sets of values, two different ideas of fairness, and two different attitudes toward each partner's career. And with each of these reminders, the couple will feel more and more like 'you and me' and less and less like 'us.' "[16]

Sarah Allen and Alan Hawkins's study of 622 mothers in dual-earner households[17] found that women who answered yes to many of the following questions were more likely to inhibit their husband's involvement in housework, despite a wish that he do more.

➤ I frequently redo some household tasks my partner hasn't done well.

➤ It's too hard to teach family members the skills necessary to do the jobs right, so I'd rather do them myself.

➤ My partner doesn't really know how to do a lot of the household chores—so it's just easier if I do them.

➤ I have higher standards than my partner for how well cared for the house should be.

➤ I like being in charge when it comes to domestic responsibilities.

➤ If visitors dropped by unexpectedly and my house was a mess, I would be embarrassed.

➤ I believe that people make judgments about how good a wife/mother I am based on how well cared for my house and kids are.

➤ I care about what my neighbors, extended family, and friends think about the way I perform my household tasks.

➤ I believe that most women enjoy caring for their homes, and men just don't like that stuff.

➤ I believe that for a lot of reasons, it's harder for men than for women to do housework and child care.

According to their findings, if you answered yes to many of the above statements you may be directly contributing to your husband's lack of participation in housework.

PATH FOR CHANGE

State your expectations clearly: Here's a list of everything that I'm doing in the course of a week. How about if you draw up a list as well and we'll compare notes.

or:

Here's a list of everything I'm doing in a week. How about if you choose two of those and commit to do them without my bugging you. I'll try not to supervise too closely.

Make trades: If you could commit to doing at least three things on my list, I'll commit to do something (of equal value) that is important to you. (Remember that you're already feeling overworked so don't make trades that aren't win/wins.)

Acknowledge how your internal conflict may be making him confused about what you want: I know that I might send you mixed messages about what I want you to do. I really do want you to take charge more in the parenting department and I'll try to not to give you so much instruction.

AN EGALITARIAN COUPLE:

•

Louise and Ned

Egalitarian couples share the belief that family work should be divided equally. Jay Belsky found that the egalitarian men in his study were typically well educated, secure, and easygoing.

Unlike traditional men, they took great pride and pleasure in their wives' careers, and in the qualities that enabled her to do her job. Egalitarian wives were typically well educated, assertive, and ambitious.[18]

These descriptions were true of Louise and Ned. Louise and Ned were both software designers who met at a large Silicon Valley company. Each headed their own division for the corporation. Louise received her master's degree in electrical engineering from the University of California at Berkeley while Ned held a degree from a small private college on the East Coast. When they decided to have children, they both agreed to an equal division of labor in parenting and housework. Ned was dutifully egalitarian with housework and strove to maintain that value toward parenting once their daughter arrived. However, once their daughter was born, Ned became far less invested in a clean house, choosing to use his small reserves of energy to play guitar or try out new programs on his computer. Louise resented this decrease in standards on Ned's part because it felt like a betrayal of their agreement prior to children.

Linda Haas found that the establishment of an equal division of chores was the most common problem in her study of egalitarian couples. She also found that couples tended to do tasks that were most in line with their gender.[19] Thus, men were more likely to maintain the car, tend to the yard, or do house maintenance while women were more likely to do housework, and to be involved in organizing the children's activities. In addition, they often had disagreements about standards, though the wives were reluctant to delegate domestic responsibility. Many wives expressed anxiety or reluctance over dealing with nontraditional roles such as talking to mechanics and service people. Over half of the people in the study voiced conflict between their jobs and family responsibility.

Most of the time, egalitarian couples coped by the *wives lowering their expectations, and the husbands raising theirs.* Most couples had to spend time experimenting and arguing before they came to some kind of resolution to their differences.[20] Daniels and Weingarten found that the traditional roles of mother as nurturer and father as playmate were far less pronounced when parents shared equally in the parenting and housekeeping roles. In those households, mothering and fathering tended to look more similar for the man and woman than they did in more traditional households.[21]

Not every couple, however, falls neatly into the categories of traditional, transitional, or egalitarian. Often couples are mixed in terms of their views. In the next section, we'll look at some of these "mixed" marriages.

TRADITIONAL MAN AND
A TRANSITIONAL WOMAN:

•

Evelyn and Dave

Our traditional couple, Lynn and Robert, had a good marriage. Lynn's husband, Robert, was very much in love with her and motivated to make her satisfied. She could count on this in her negotiations with him, and know that he had a fundamental desire to see her happy, even if he disagreed with her.

Lynn's sister, Evelyn, wasn't so fortunate in her choice of husbands. Like Lynn, Evelyn was raised with the expectation and desire for a traditional family. However, unlike Lynn's husband, Evelyn's husband, Dave, refused to do anything other than go to his job. When their lawn got out of control, Evelyn felt forced to mow it herself to avoid the embarrassment of letting it get any higher. In addition to being a full-time parent and homemaker, she felt obligated to take on a lot of nontraditional tasks such as taking care of the car or doing basic household repairs.

Little in Evelyn's life had prepared her for the negotiating and bargaining skills she needed to deal with a man like Dave. She grew up observing a mother who deferred to her husband and was passive in most of her dealings with him. In addition, Evelyn's lack of financial independence made it harder for her to feel as if she could play the divorce card if she had to.

Marital conflict and the need to change the workload can sometimes transform the belief system of one or both members of a couple. While Evelyn grew up expecting a traditional marriage, events in her own marriage moved her in the direction of wanting to have more power in her relationship with Dave. Among other decisions, the stresses in her marriage caused Evelyn to consider getting a job. However, her decision to go to work had implications for the marriage that neither had anticipated, not least of which was how much conflict it would generate.

For example, Evelyn's decision to get a job threatened Dave's identity as a man. When he told his brother that his wife was thinking about getting a job, his brother teased him by saying, "Damn, Dave, pretty soon she's gonna have you doing the laundry! Honey, I'm home! Did you wash my bra and panties?" Dave wasn't amused. As his brother's joke implied, Evelyn's employment meant that he was less of a man in the world.

Dave was angry at Evelyn for changing their arrangement from the type in which they both grew up. Her decision to get a job meant not only a change in her definition of herself but also a change in how he got to define himself as a man.

WHAT'S EVELYN TO DO?

Evelyn may be able to sidestep this problematic dynamic with Dave if she doesn't let their discussions deteriorate into a blamefest. She should tell him that she wants to go to work in order to make a greater contribution to the family, that most families these days require two incomes, and that she'll be a happier person as a result. She should reassure him that her getting a job isn't a reflection of his adequacy as a husband or man. This conversation might go something like this:

EVELYN: I'm thinking of getting a job.

DAVE: What for? We don't need the money.

E: I know, I'm just wanting more money to spend on what I want. Besides, I need to get out of the house more.

D: What about the kids?

E: My mom said she'd help.

D: Nah. We don't need you working. I don't like it. I never wanted my wife to have to work.

E: That's my point, I don't have to. I want to.

D: I still don't like it.

E: Well, I want to be respectful of your feelings. I really do. On the other hand, I want you to respect mine, too. Let's both keep thinking about it and talking about it for the next few weeks.

D: I don't need to think about it, I already made up my mind.

E: Well, I don't want this to be a power struggle between us. It's just something that's important for me to do for me.

D: I forbid it.

E: Dave, you can't forbid it. I'm an adult. I want to be sensitive to your feelings but we're both grown-ups here.

In this scenario, Evelyn tries to contain the conflict as a way to decrease his feeling threatened, something that may be a challenging task. While containing or managing conflict is important in any marriage, *it's also important to not be so conflict averse that you get locked into unproductive stances.*[22] Therefore, if Dave remains inflexible, Evelyn may have to move the conversation into a more overt conflict. This conversation may go something like this:

Several weeks later . . .

E: So have you thought any more about my getting a job?

D: No, I already told you my decision.

E: Well, we have a conflict, then, because I've decided that it's something I'm gonna do.

D: Over my dead body.

E: Dave, don't make this a power struggle. You're putting me in a position where you're saying I don't have a right to live my life in the way that I want.

D: No, I'm not. When you and I got married, you said that you wanted to be a stay-at-home mom and now you're changing the rules on me and I don't like it one bit.

E: You're right, I did say that, and I could see why you'd be confused and mad about it. But I don't think either of us knew what it was going to be like—I certainly didn't. I also never agreed that being a homemaker meant that I'd have to do a bunch of the stuff that most men do like yard work, taking care of the cars, or fixing things. I mean, I appreciate the financial support you provide, but everything else falls on me and it's burning me out.

D: So how is getting a job supposed to change any of that?

E: Well, I could hire people to do some of the things you're not doing. I could be away from the house more, which I think would be good for me. We'd have more money to do some of the things we've both wanted to do, like take a vacation.

D: I still don't like it.

E: I understand that. I hope you can respect my wishes on this. Let's do it for at least six months and then see where we are.

Evelyn's suggestion that she get a job on a trial basis is a good bargaining technique because it makes the decision less final. It implies that there may be an opportunity for Dave to assert his influence at a later date, a fact that may be important to his identity as a man. In addition, neither of them knows whether Evelyn's decision to work outside the home will be a good or a bad thing. She may discover that it's harder for her to be away from her children than she thought, and that the gain may not outweigh the pain. She may also find that the increase in conflict with Dave doesn't outweigh the benefits of the job. On the other hand, Dave may like the increase in income and its benefits to the family; he may also like the increase in well-being that it produces in his wife. Neither of them may know until there's been a trial period of Evelyn working.

Either way, Dave is going to have to readjust his worldview in order to successfully accommodate the changes in Evelyn, and this may be a bitter pill for him to swallow. Ideally, she would be both empathetic to Dave's objections and immune enough to his anger to implement the independence and changes that she wants. One of her challenges will be managing the guilt and anxiety she feels about transitioning from an identity as a homemaker to being a member of the workforce. Her own family background may also make her more vulnerable to accusations from Dave, his family, and her parents that she's behaving selfishly to want to stop being a full-time mom.

OTHER OPTIONS

In addition to getting a job, Evelyn has the following other options to get Dave to do more:

> ➤ **DO A "SHARING SHOWDOWN."**[23] While Evelyn is dependent on Dave financially, he is currently dependent on her to do a whole host of tasks that maintain his well-being. She should figure out what she can remove from her list that would either

get his attention or that he would be forced to assume. While Dave is less committed to Evelyn than Lynn's husband is to her, he nonetheless may be encouraged to do more through this strategy.

➤ **INCREASE HER NEGOTIATING SKILLS BY TAKING AN ASSERT-IVENESS TRAINING CLASS OR GETTING INTO PSYCHOTHER-APY.** She could also try to get Dave into couple's therapy or a marriage-based workshop so he can learn how to develop empathy toward her.

➤ **EXAMINE HOW SHE COMMUNICATES HER FEELINGS TO DAVE.** Dave may have withdrawn from Evelyn because of the way that she communicates her resentment to him. Over time, he may have withdrawn more and more as a result.[24] Thus, Evelyn should be sure that she's doing everything she can to appreciate what Dave contributes or has contributed in the past.

A TRADITIONAL MAN MARRIED TO AN EGALITARIAN WOMAN:

•

Walter and Vivian

Vivian met Walter when they were in high school. A direct and intelligent woman, Vivian liked that Walter had the same qualities. While they occasionally had debates about the roles of women and men, these differences rarely invaded their home life before children. Walter's traditional beliefs became an issue when Vivian wanted to finish her bachelor's degree after their son was three.

WALTER: *I guess we should have talked a lot more about whether she planned to be a full-time mom but I just assumed she would. I mean, you hear about women, once they have kids, that all they want is to be home with them, so I figured she'd be that way too. And now she expects me to be one of these superdads who wants to spend every waking moment with his kids on top of it? I didn't bargain for that.*

While not especially common,[25] a traditional man and an egalitarian woman may coexist without a lot of turmoil before children come on the scene. However, there's nothing like the arrival of children to bring the differences in views about men's and women's roles into sharp focus. This is because an egalitarian woman believes her husband should do half of the parenting and housework, while a traditional man believes that his wife should do almost *all* the parenting and *all* of the housework.

It's not hard to see how couples with such different standards of fairness could quickly get locked into conflict. For example, because Walter loved Vivian and wanted to make her happy, he decided to increase his efforts with the kids and cleaning from around 10 percent of participation to 25 percent. This was a huge increase in his mind. However, Vivian wasn't that thrilled because it still left her doing 75 percent of the parenting and housework.

VIVIAN: *We have the most fights around my work. That's because it's usually my job to get the boys ready for school every day, get their lunches made the night before, make sure they've done their homework, the whole nine yards. That all works okay unless I'm supposed to have an early sales meeting which my company springs on us from time to time. When that happens, I need Walter to pick up some of the slack at home, and those discussions never go well because he's so resistant to any change in his routine. So it usually means that I have to either get up early and do everything myself to make sure it gets done, have an argument with him about why he should pitch in more, or try to get the sitter to come to the house early to do all of the things that he refuses to do.*

Traditional men can also feel threatened by their lack of economic power over their employed wives.[26] Many fear that they will have less of a hold on their wife if she earns as much as or more than they. This fear isn't entirely without warrant. Women who have the financial power to leave marriages are far more likely to file for divorce than those who don't.[27] Unfortunately, when men try to assert their independence by refusing to participate in family work, this only increases the probability that their wives will entertain thoughts of divorce.[28]

A traditional man married to an egalitarian woman is the most unstable and problematic of all arrangements.[29] This is probably true because the conflict cycle goes something like this:

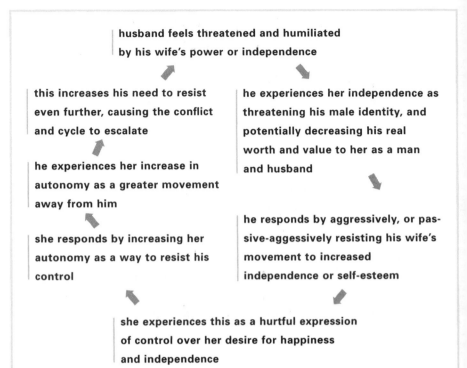

husband feels threatened and humiliated by his wife's power or independence

this increases his need to resist even further, causing the conflict and cycle to escalate

he experiences her increase in autonomy as a greater movement away from him

she responds by increasing her autonomy as a way to resist his control

he experiences her independence as threatening his male identity, and potentially decreasing his real worth and value to her as a man and husband

he responds by aggressively, or passive-aggessively resisting his wife's movement to increased independence or self-esteem

she experiences this as a hurtful expression of control over her desire for happiness and independence

Most men grew up in homes where their fathers were the primary breadwinners. As a result, few have role models of how to share income or family work. Their view of men is shaped by watching what their fathers did, and most of the time it was earning money. Thus, even men who have beliefs that income and family work should be shared equally can feel inadequate if their wives earn as much as or more than do they.

Because men are so often judged by other men in terms of their income and careers, even nontraditional men can feel inadequate if they're not the primary or sole providers. I commonly hear men in my practice express embarrassment when they can't afford to do what they would like for their wives or children such as go on a vacation, buy a new car, or fix the house. In other words, our belief systems can offer only so much protection against the cultural forces that tell men what they should be providing for their families in order to be men.

Some women feel guilty that their husbands feel threatened by their income or status, and then compensate by being supermoms and superwives when they're home.[30] In these households, she attempts to restore the husband's loss of power by maintaining the same domestic workload she would have if she weren't employed outside the home. Unfortunately, this reinforces the dynamic of her doing more than her fair share.

A far less common arrangement is a traditional woman married to a man who is more egalitarian in his outlook. This is generally a less conflictual arrangement because these husbands contribute more to family work and that's typically a net gain for women. Why would they object? Those who object may do so because they experience their husband's involvement in domestic affairs as a thrust into their area of expertise and competence. In those households, women may resent or feel threatened by their husbands' desire to share family work equally. In addition, an egalitarian man may expect his wife to work outside the home, something a traditional woman may well oppose.

TRANSITIONAL MAN
AND AN EGALITARIAN WOMAN:
•
June and Frank

Most men today behave in a manner somewhere between traditional and egalitarian.[31] Problems often arise when a transitional man is married to an egalitarian woman because, while a transitional man believes he should do 25 to 35 percent of the family work (a full 10 to 35 percent more than the traditional man) his wife believes he should do closer to 50 percent.[32] This leaves a 15 to 25 percent difference in their beliefs about how much each should do. That's a percentage difference large enough to drive a truck through in most homes.

> **JUNE:** *Frank's a good guy and a good dad but he acts like he's doing me a personal favor whenever he washes a dish or spends time with the boys. He calls it baby-sitting when he takes care of them, which gets on my nerves. I always say, "No, Frank, baby-sitting is what the neighbor's high school daughter does. What you do is called* parenting."

Frank has a different perspective.

> **FRANK:** *I know June complains if it's not exactly fifty-fifty but I feel like, give me a break, I do so much more than my father did or any other guy in my family ever did. I mean, I'm not perfect, but most guys I know don't do half of what I do. I would like a little more credit.*

While June grants that Frank does more than a lot of men, she doesn't believe that this entitles him to a lot of gratitude for something that is still less than half. June is bugged by Frank's attitudes because she doesn't like being put into the position of household manager. June says, "If either of the kids get sick, I'm the one who misses work even though I earn as much as him. It's this expectation that just because I'm the woman it's all up to me, that's the part that gets on my nerves."

The difference in their beliefs about responsibilities also caused conflict when June wanted to return to her family law practice after a six-month maternity leave. Frank expressed concern.

> *I just felt like, our daughter's only four months old, I'm not that comfortable leaving her with the nanny for big stretches of time. It isn't like I don't think I could or even should cut back on my work to be home with her, it's just that I don't think it would be as good for the baby to be home with me or the nanny. I feel like I can make a bigger contribution at this point with income than with child care, while she can make the most unique contribution by being a mother.*

Here again, his belief as a transitional man that *mothers are irreplaceable* is in conflict with her belief as an egalitarian woman that *a father can do just as good a job as a mother*.

PATH FOR CHANGE

If you're an egalitarian woman married to a transitional man consider the following recommendations:

➤ **ERR ON THE SIDE OF APPRECIATION.** While it's absolutely reasonable to expect a full 50 percent contribution, you have to work with who you married. The reality is that you married someone whom you either knew was transitional or his belief system got revealed with the arrival of kids, as happens in so many families. In either event, you should begin with what he's doing right, and make that your platform, not what he's doing wrong. A conversation on this topic might go something like this:

JUNE: *I really appreciate how much you do around the house and with the kids. I know you do a lot more than you dad ever did, and you also do more than most of the other men out there. However, I'd like to talk about how we're delegating the chores here because too much is falling on me.*

As you can see in the above example, June leads with the reality that Frank is 1) already doing a lot and 2) doing more than other men. If she sidesteps those realities and goes straight to the reality that she's doing more than he is (and more than her mother did) the conversation will quickly become unproductive. Once she has his interest, she can begin to use any of the principles mentioned with Evelyn and Dave such as a sharing showdown, bargaining, making trade-offs, etc.

➤ **YOU DON'T HAVE TO CAVE IN ON THE THINGS THAT MATTER THE MOST TO YOU.** Many women have a hard enough time managing their own guilt about returning to work without having to fend off their husband's accusations or suggestions that they're not doing enough for their children. It's your perfect right to return to full-time employment, and your husband shouldn't try to make you feel as though you're being selfish or neglectful for it. That said, if you do carry some feelings of guilt or worry about it, then his statements or anyone else's have the potential to ignite a powder keg of conflict between the two of you. The worst fights are always those that invade the areas where we feel the most guilt-ridden. Therefore you may need additional support from friends if this is one of those areas for you.

Either way, it's important to come to an arrangement that you can feel good about. As psychologists and family researchers Carolyn and Philip Cowan write, "Neither the traditional male/female division nor the new egalitarian sharing arrangements stand out as ideal. Modern couples get penalized either way. When one parent brings home the bacon while the other stays home to look after the child, both can feel underappreciated and strapped economically, which burdens the marriage and the children. When both parents work outside the family, they tend to feel better about themselves and about their contributions to the family economy, but parents and children are breathless, often missing the opportunity for intimate moments. Although each of these alternatives has costs and benefits, we find that when men are more involved in the care of their children, they feel better about themselves, their wives feel better about themselves, and they both feel better about their marriage. Even more important than who actually does what is how the arrangements are negotiated and how both partners feel about the outcome."[33]

On the basis of the examples in this chapter, how would you describe your marriage?

    We're both traditional.

    We're both transitional.

We're both egalitarian.

I'm traditional, he's transitional or egalitarian.

I'm transitional, he's egalitarian or traditional.

I'm egalitarian, he's transitional or traditional.

How might you be contributing to your husband's lack of participation?

I give too much direction or want too much control.

My standards are too high.

I'm too critical of what he does with the house or kids.

I'm not assertive enough.

I'm conflicted about what's fair or not fair to ask, demand, or expect.

It's easier to just do everything myself.

What psychological obstacle may be preventing you from getting your husband to do more?

my guilt

my anger

my ambivalence

my fear of his reactions

my fear of other people's reactions such as my parents or my friends

my frustration or impatience

my ego

Your comfort with using your strength and assertiveness is often shaped by the family in which you grew up. In the next few chapters, we'll look at how the messages from your parents affect how you communicate and what you feel entitled to demand in marriage. Communicating productively is critical when trying to get someone to do something they don't want to do. Sometimes it's a matter of talking softly, other times it's a matter of carrying a big stick, and other times it's a matter of talking softly *and* carrying a big stick.

Childhood Revisited

Every marriage is influenced by the childhood in which one grows up. If you were raised in a home where there was lousy communication between your parents, verbal or physical abuse, ongoing hostility, or divorce, there is a much greater chance that you've brought some of those qualities into your marriage.[1] Likewise, if your parents were unaffectionate in their marriage, or with you, you may not be the most touchy-feely person to ever walk across a bedroom floor.

The impact of our childhood can come to the surface after we become parents because the increase in workload and the decrease in "me time" may remind us of how little we received from our own parents, or remind us of the pain that we experienced when we were children.[2]

ALICIA: *I was terrified of how innocent and vulnerable my baby was when I first saw her. My first thought was,* Oh my God, that was me at one point. *It was a big reminder of how alone and unprotected I felt growing up with my mother. I got scared that I wouldn't be able to be a better mom than mine, which is really important to me.*

Understanding your childhood is crucial to your well-being and to getting your husband to do more. This is because our ability to communicate is strongly influenced by what we observed and how we were treated when we were young. Your past can also affect the amount of strength or affection you are able to bring to your marriage. Ideally, we bring a healthy balance of both of those qualities to the altar. In reality, people usually suffer from too much strength or too little of it. This chapter will look at how the past may be affecting your present. We'll look at how you and your partner are both being affected by your childhoods and examine how to use this knowledge to create a better arrangement between the two of you.

The Entitled and the Unentitled

Because women are socialized to be more empathic and understanding, they're more likely to err on the side of giving in, and then getting walked on or ignored.[3] Men, on the other hand, are socialized to be on the self-interested end of the continuum. While I sometimes meet husbands who need to work on being more assertive, men more commonly need to work on being more sensitive and accommodating to their partners.

Of course, it's rarely simple. People are sometimes the most difficult when they fear that they won't be taken seriously, or when they believe they don't have enough power to affect the other. In those situations, their "strength" becomes the problem.

> YONI: *My mother waited on my father hand and foot, but that was true of all of my friends' moms. What I couldn't*

stand was how my mother let him treat her like crap. It's one thing to be the dutiful wife, it's another to not have any respect for yourself. So I vowed I'd never let a man treat me the way my dad treated her and I've lived up to that.

While Yoni had been successful in choosing a man who loved her, she had taken the lesson from childhood so much to heart that it made her approach her husband in a combative fashion. In couple's therapy, she spoke to him much in the same shaming, belittling way that I imagine her father spoke to her mother. While getting mad at times is understandable if not unavoidable, Yoni's daily communication in this style made her husband shut down and withdraw. Over time, she learned to communicate in a less critical way, and he became more interested in how overwhelmed she felt with the house and kids, and committed to change.

Why would Yoni's changing her communication have such a profound effect on her husband's motivation? Because no one changes with a gun to his head, at least not for very long. Lasting change in marriage occurs when people *want* to make their partner happy. Most people respond to criticism by feeling shamed, humiliated, or rejected and react to those feelings by shutting down and withdrawing, or hurling the criticisms back. Neither produces much of anything very productive.

On the other hand, just being nice doesn't always get it. Harriet came from a background similar to Yoni's, with a mom who did everything and a father who was uninvolved and critical of her mother. Rather than adopting a first-strike policy, as did Yoni, Harriet identified with her mother and became passive and withdrawn in her marriage. Harriet needed to learn how to become more assertive with her requests for help and participation. Over time, she had to develop the strength to take on her husband and not feel so afraid of his objections or complaints.

> **HARRIET**: *I was pretty timid for the first five years of my marriage. If William raised his voice, I'd clam up just to make sure it didn't escalate in the way my parents' fights always would. For the longest time I thought that if I was just nice enough and didn't make waves that he'd see what I needed or how bad he made me feel. That was pretty naive. It's taken me years, but I've learned that I have much better luck getting him to do what I want by being stronger rather than nicer. I'm not a bitch, I just know when to let him know that I mean business.*

A Critical Parent

Critical comments can sometimes be more exasperating (and damaging) when they come from our own parents. And they can also feel more difficult to ignore. In the last chapter we saw that Penny has to become stronger in order to deal with her mother-in-law. Part of the reason that Penny struggles so much is because she grew up with parents who were shaming and belittling of her. As a result, she goes through life trying hard to fend off others' judgments of her. A good deal of her energy goes toward trying to please others rather than to creating happiness or well-being in herself.

Growing up with critical parents can make you either too critical of others or too intimidated by them.[4] Penny tends to err on the side of feeling too intimidated. As a result, she believes she has to keep her house spotless to avoid others' judgments. In addition, her fear of others' criticisms causes her to be too passive in her dealings with her husband. He consciously or unconsciously knows that if he raises his voice with her or acts upset about her requests for his involvement that she'll back off. In other words, Penny's enslavement to her fear of criticism restricts her freedom of movement with both her husband and her in-laws. It causes her to prioritize activities that she might not were she more free of their real or imagined judgment.

Penny would be helped on this issue by learning to adopt the following beliefs:

> I have a right to run my house and family in the way that
> I see fit.
> I can tolerate others' judgments of me.
> It's harmful to me to be too concerned about what others
> think.
> I have a right to a happy and relaxed life.

Penny also needs to work on her beliefs that she's supposed to give more in life than receive. While many women have been socialized with this belief, others are further affected by being raised in homes where their parents reinforced it. For example, you may have developed this belief as a result of being raised by parents who were depressed, needy, or self-centered. This could have left you believing that others' needs are more important than yours. When children are raised in this type of household, they are more likely to feel excessively guilt-ridden or obligated to be sensitive to others' feelings in a way that compromises their well-being.

VERONICA: *Both of my parents were pretty depressed. I think I basically raised myself. It made me a stronger person in some ways, but I don't think it taught me very much about how to give to myself, or make demands of others.*

Veronica has a hard time knowing what she needs or knowing when to state her needs. Because her parents required so much caretaking when she was a child, she developed the belief that her needs are less important than others'. This greatly weakens her power with her husband and teenage sons who don't seem to share her selflessness. It leaves her vulnerable to being taken advantage of and being taken for granted. Her sons and husband well know that if they leave their messes, mom will clean them up. In addition, they know that if they complain long or loud enough about her demands that they do more, she'll cave in and do it herself. While some part of Veronica knows this is unfair to her (not to mention ineffective parenting), she is enslaved by a belief that she's supposed to give more in life than are others. This is especially challenging for her since she is living with three males who don't suffer from such an unentitled belief system.

As a way to consider how your childhood could be affecting your marriage and your bargaining power, consider the following questions:

How did your mother treat your father? Was she:
    affectionate
    involved
    unaffectionate
    uninvolved
    critical

blaming

shaming

rejecting

loving

In what ways are you similar to her?

What were her strengths and weaknesses?

What might you have concluded about how men should be treated on the basis of observing your mother with your father? For example:
Men should be pampered and waited on.
Men need to be yelled at to get them to do anything.
Men should be ignored.
Men are useless.
If you want something done right, do it yourself.
Men will hurt you if you're not careful.

How did your father treat your mother? Was he:
affectionate
involved
unaffectionate
uninvolved
critical
blaming
shaming
rejecting
loving

In what ways are you similar to him?

What were his strengths and weaknesses?

**What might you have concluded about how women should
be treated on the basis of this? For example:**
> Women should serve men.
> Women are inferior.
> Women are more powerful than men.
> Women are more vulnerable.

How did your mother treat you? Was she:
> affectionate
> involved
> unaffectionate
> uninvolved
> critical
> blaming
> shaming
> rejecting
> loving

**What might have you concluded about what you deserve
in life on the basis of her treatment of you? For
example:**
> I deserve respect.
> I'm going to be rejected.
> If people get to know me they won't like me.
> I need to protect myself and not let anyone hurt me.

How did your father treat you? **Was he:**
affectionate
involved
unaffectionate
uninvolved
critical
blaming
shaming
rejecting
loving

What might you have concluded about what you deserve in life on the basis of his treatment of you? For example:
I deserve respect.
I'm going to be rejected.
If people get to know me they won't like me.
I need to protect myself and not let anyone hurt me.

If you were raised without contact with one of your parents, what did you conclude about his or her lack of involvement with you? For example:
I'm not very important.
I don't deserve love.
It's not safe to trust anyone.
I can do a lot without anyone's help.
I'm strong.

What areas do you need to work on in your communication with your husband? I should:
be more patient
be less critical

not yell as much

be more direct

not avoid conflict so much

appreciate him more

What would you like him to work on? I want him to:

be more patient with me

be less critical

not yell as much

be more direct

not avoid conflict as much

appreciate me more

Exercises

Write out a list of all of the changes you'd like to see in your life. Divide these into as many categories as needed. Begin with "changes in myself," then "changes in my marriage," and go from there. Some common examples are "changes in my family," "changes at work," "changes in relations with in-laws," "changes in my relationship with my friends."

Make a commitment to choose one or two from each category and work on them for the next six months. Veronica's list was as follows:

CHANGE IN SELF:

work on prioritizing my own needs

increase my assertiveness

take at least one day to respond before I agree to take on
    any new responsibilities or tasks with my family or work

ask myself if I'm agreeing to do something because it's good or valuable for me, or if I'm doing it so I don't feel guilty

work on the amount of guilt I feel when I say no to others

CHANGE IN MARRIAGE:

Get my husband to do more parenting and housework by:

changing my standards

increasing my assertiveness

increasing my bargaining power

working on my belief that I'm supposed to give more than receive.

FIND YOUR RESILIENCE:

People who grow up in abusive homes often feel fragile and vulnerable. This is because they're ruled by a belief system that constantly tells them:

People will get you if you're not careful.

I'm alone in this world.

I don't deserve love or respect. If I'm going to get respect, it's because I make people give it to me.

I can't tolerate getting hurt; it's catastrophic to get rejected or ignored.

It's better to victimize others than to let myself get victimized.

Don't trust anybody, you'll just get hurt.

If they're afraid of you they're less likely to hurt you or take advantage of you.

This belief system contributes to a feeling of vulnerability, anxiety, and fragility. In order to change, you will have to work directly on how your childhood affected how you think and feel about yourself. Changing your state of mind, let alone your behavior, requires conscious engagement with your critical and fearful thoughts. Many people resist doing affirmations because they seem too New Age or contrived. What they don't realize are the ways that they're engaging in a daily affirmation of self-torment. Active confrontation of those negative beliefs can be useful in combating your tendency to unconsciously affirm your dysfunctional beliefs.

SOME EXAMPLES OF POSITIVE
AFFIRMATIONS ARE:

I deserve love and respect.

I have the resources to change.

It's not a catastrophe if I get hurt.

I deserve to feel good about myself even if I make mistakes.

In this chapter we have begun to look at how childhood affects communication and a sense of self. In the next chapter, we'll continue this discussion by looking at different personality types and how those contribute to problems or solutions around parenting and housework. Laziness is a matter of perspective. It may be that you let your husband off the hook too easily in regard to his contributions or that your expectations are unfair. It's sometimes hard to know until you begin to have an ongoing and productive dialogue with him about his beliefs, expectations, and values regarding the house and children.

It's a Personality Thing

Most of us are unaware of the many subtle, obnoxious, provocative, rejecting, and undermining behaviors we participate in on a daily basis that contribute to the problems in our marriages. When I went into couple's therapy when my children were young, I couldn't wait to have the therapist show my wife the error of her ways. I assumed it would go something like this:

> **THERAPIST**: *Well, I think your husband is completely right and you're completely wrong. If you simply change everything that he's telling you to change, and if you don't talk or think about the things you want him to change, you should be able to live happily ever after. Now, that wasn't so hard, was it? That will be one hundred and fifty dollars.*

While your partner may be the problem, you may be a bigger problem than you realize. Or you're enough of the problem that working on yourself can bring a change to the whole system.[1] A key part of creating change in a marriage comes from gaining an understanding of how your and your partner's personalities affect your marriage. So continuing with where we left off in the last chapter, you need to know how your past

> ➤ makes you reactive to certain types of behavior or communication from him
> ➤ contributes to your misperceiving him
> ➤ makes you behave in ways that are confusing or troubling to him.

In addition to understanding your past, it's equally important that you know and understand how his past

> ➤ makes him react to certain types of behavior or communication from you
> ➤ contributes to his misperceiving you
> ➤ makes him behave in ways that are confusing or troubling to you

Understanding his personality and how he got to be that way is empowering because it can help you correct his misperceptions about you, and help you to communicate in ways that don't trigger his anxiety, negativity, or defensiveness. This chapter will look at common personality types, how they can create problems, and how to create change. These are The Boy-Husband, The Worried Wife, The Worried Husband, The Perfectionistic Wife, The Perfectionistic Husband, The Angry Husband, and the Angry Wife.

The Boy-Husband

Bob was twenty-six and working at an electronics store as a floor salesman when he met his wife, Lana. It was his third job in a year. He had lost his prior jobs as a result of either tardiness or poor work performance. Bob was attracted to Lana in part because she had all of the qualities that he didn't possess, such as being responsible and earning a good income. Lana was drawn to Bob because of his sense of humor and his kindness. Bob was also an aspiring singer-songwriter and his artistic side also appealed to her. She believed him when he said that he had a string of bad luck with his jobs, and that he had big plans with his music.

Bob had grown up in a household with two depressed and ineffective parents. Both his mother and father used excessive amounts of pot and alcohol and did little in the way of supervising him or his older sister. While Bob's parents weren't cruel, they also weren't involved in any meaningful way in helping him plan, structure, or organize his life. His sister, Clara, dropped out of high school when she was sixteen and moved to the East Coast with her boyfriend. Bob barely finished high school. When he met Lana he was living with several childhood friends in a run-down apartment on the outskirts of the city.

While Lana was correct in her perception that Bob was a good person, she had no idea how incapable he was of conducting an adult life when she married him. She had to wake him up every morning to make sure he wasn't late for work, and was shocked to learn that he spent most of his paychecks on CDs or eating out. Lana decided that the best way to prevent Bob from dragging them into the poorhouse was to take over his money and his bills.

This was fine with Bob. He knew he needed help managing his life and was more than willing to have someone else run it for him. When Lana became pregnant, he wasn't sure if they could afford a child, but figured that if Lana wasn't worried about it, he didn't need to be either. Lana mistakenly assumed that the increase in responsibility of parenthood would serve as a shock treatment to Bob's indolence and force him to grow up and change.

JUST ONE MORE CHILD TO TAKE CARE OF

I commonly hear women complain that living with their husband is like having another child. Sometimes this is an unfair accusation because many men assume responsibility in ways that benefit women and children, even if they're not the responsibilities that women would prefer. In Lana's case, she was right to complain that Bob was like another child. While Lana benefited from Bob's affectionate and easygoing nature, over time she began to resent how much she had to do to make his life run smoothly.

If these behaviors describe your partner, consider the following guidelines:

WORK TO FEEL LESS RESPONSIBLE FOR HIM

Become aware of the origins of your feelings of overresponsibility and work toward being more detached from those feelings. Women are socialized to feel responsible for others, and many have a harder time feeling happy if their husband or children are distressed in any way.[2] While I'm not advocating a cold detachment, an affectionate detachment can do wonders. Taking another page from parenting advice, *allow natural consequences to occur in your partner's life.* In Lana's case, she was fearful that if she didn't make Bob get out of bed in the morning, he'd get fired. And right she was. However, Lana had to decide whether she wanted Bob to really grow up or remain a third dependent. She had to let Bob clearly know that she wasn't going to continue to parent him.

GAIN AN UNDERSTANDING OF WHY YOU ARE OVERLY RESPONSIBLE

A dependent husband can only continue his dependence if he's being supported by his wife. Her acceptance of this behavior often exists because of an unregulated feeling of responsibility on her part. For example, Lana was the eldest child in a family of seven. At a young age, she developed the capacity to competently have five activities going at once. Making Bob's life run smoothly was just one more unchallenging item on a daily list.

It wasn't until her first child that she began to feel the drag of Bob's dependency. Unfortunately, by then, they were firmly entrenched in a pattern for which Lana had to take equal responsibility. She married Bob knowing that he wasn't very evolved in the responsibility department, and she also perpetuated the pattern by agreeing to run aspects of his life that he should have been running himself.

In order to determine how much your feelings of over-responsibility contribute to your husband's laziness, see how many of the following statements are true for you:

I have a harder time receiving than giving.

I feel burdened by how much time I spend worrying about my spouse.

My husband often complains that I'm too intrusive in his life, but if I'm not, all hell would break loose.

I feel exhausted all the time because I'm constantly over-committing myself.

I feel guilty if the people closest to me are struggling.

If I can help someone I'm close to, I will, even if it's at my own expense.

I don't know how to relax and have fun.

USE NONJUDGMENTAL LANGUAGE TO LET YOUR PARTNER KNOW OF YOUR CHANGE

If you're planning a new regimen, it's a good idea to give your partner notice without humiliating him. In Lana's case, she had to take responsibility for the fact that she was an equal party to their dynamic. She married Bob knowing he had a hard time managing adult responsibilities. It would be unfair for her to suddenly decide that Bob is an inadequate person because of his inability to manage responsibility. She could have easily shamed and humiliated him by announcing that she wasn't going to play mommy anymore with him.

Bearing this in mind, I advised her to structure a dialogue in the following way:

LANA: I've been thinking about our division of labor and would like to try something different. It worked okay before the kids were born to help you with organization because I had a lot more time. However, I'm feeling really exhausted and am looking for ways to decrease my stress load. So I'd like to talk with you about your taking over some of the things you could probably do without my help. What do you think?

BOB: Such as?

LANA: Making you get out of bed in the morning, making your lunch. Doing all of the bill paying.

BOB: That's fine, I just might lose my job if you don't wake me up because you know how hard it is for me to get out of bed.

LANA: I'm happy to go with you to buy a louder alarm clock.

BOB: And bill paying? You know I don't even know how to balance my checkbook.

LANA: I don't mind balancing the checkbooks, but it doesn't take any great skill to write checks and put them in envelopes. Let's set up a system sometime this week for you to take it over. I'm open to trading something else that you could take care of in exchange. I just don't want to take on as much as I have been.

Lana could begin her new regimen by discontinuing the task of getting Bob out of bed in the mornings and making his lunch. If she decides that bill paying is something she really wants him to assume, that may require a little more shepherding. In general, I recommend a graduated instituting of activities where you slowly phase out of the tasks you want him to take over. Remember, if taking on these responsibilities is something he's never done, he may *truly* feel terrified, confused, or over-whelmed by the prospect of adding these new behaviors to his regimen. It may not just be a manipulation when he says he doesn't know how.

MAKE AN HONEST ASSESSMENT OF WHETHER SOME PART OF YOU LIKES OR BENEFITS FROM YOUR PARTNER'S DEPENDENCY

For example, if you were rejected and devalued as a child, you may be reassured by your husband's neediness or even incompetence. This may cause you to subtly undermine him through teasing, criticizing, or shaming. It may make you focus excessively on what he's doing wrong and ignore what he's doing right. If this is the case, strive to recognize that part of yourself and begin to shift your attention to the positive aspects of your partner's behavior or contributions.

The other reason for having a conversation about your partner's dependence is that the dependent person, rightly or wrongly, often believes that his partner *likes* his dependency. For example, Wesley grew up in eastern Pennsylvania with a single mother who was fearful and dependent. She was possessive of Wesley and ambivalent about his becoming an independent person because it meant that he would leave her. His mother was critical of all of his girlfriends in high school and college and constantly tried to undermine his wife when he finally married in his forties.

Wesley, like Bob, never learned how to be a fully functioning adult. He was gifted intellectually, but always got C's and dropped out of college two semesters before getting his bachelor's degree. While Bob's dependency stemmed from parental neglect, Wesley's stemmed from a powerful belief that others don't want him to be independent. Because his mother was clearly threatened by his independence, Wesley came to believe that behaving in an independent manner is hurtful to others. When his wife didn't challenge his dependency, he assumed (wrongly) that it was because she liked and benefited from it, much as his mother did when he was younger.

Note

➤It's important to use loving confrontation and limit setting around the behavior of someone who's functioning well beneath his abilities. However, you're not doing him any favor by accepting his excuses and running his life for him. Your taking over communicates that he can't learn how to be independent and run his own life. Neither of these beliefs contribute much to adult happiness or satisfaction.

DON'T EXPECT OVERNIGHT CHANGE

If someone has traveled all the way into adulthood without being able to successfully manage adult responsibilities or having learned how to take advantage of unrealized potential, they're not going to change overnight. It's more likely to take some time for them to successfully turn it around. What *can* change overnight is how much *you* do for your partner that he can rightly do for himself. This is important because phasing out your role of overresponsibility can free up time and resources that you can apply to activities more to your liking. And it may be that his doing even a little more will decrease your resentment and increase your affection.

Note

➤ People sometimes behave irresponsibly because they have attention deficit disorder (ADD). ADD can make an otherwise competent person look like a complete mess. Common characteristics of ADD are the following:[3]

➤ inability to complete tasks
➤ difficulties organizing, planning, or following through
➤ messy, easily overwhelmed
➤ easily burdened by routine tasks such as filling out forms
➤ problems with impulse control
➤ enjoys risk-taking behavior
➤ difficulties transitioning from one activity to next
➤ may look or feel as if they're run by a motor

If this describes you or your husband, contact your doctor for a referral to a specialist. Proper medication and treatment can make a huge difference.

The Worried Wife

Worry is often at the core of overly responsible behavior. For example, Liya refused to get baby-sitting despite the fact that her twins were over three years of age.

When they came to see me in couple's therapy, her husband was furious at her because she'd never go out on a date with him without the children in tow. In discussing this, Liya confessed that she was terrified of leaving the children with a baby-sitter due to the occasional stories about child abductions or abuse. In order to save her marriage, Liya needed to begin to learn how to tolerate leaving the children with baby-sitters.

We first worked to determine who would be a trustworthy sitter and then followed up with small steps. The first night with the sitter, they went out for an hour to a café in the neighborhood—close enough for them to return if there was an emergency (which Liya assumed was a high probability). As Liya became more confident over the next six months, they were gradually able to extend the length of time and distance that they were away from the children. Within a year, she was able to go away for a weekend without being terrified or guilt-ridden.

If worry is a dominant feature of your emotional landscape, you may be helped to set goals around it and then proceed in stepwise fashion. You should also consider a medication evaluation if you feel greatly burdened by your worries. Being a worrier can cause your husband to tune you out. A part of getting him to do more may mean becoming less worried so that he actually wants to hear what you have to say.

WHAT TO DO IF THIS DESCRIBES YOU

Strive to understand the nature of your worry. Ask yourself the following questions:

Does it appear rational?

Did something happen in my childhood or past that has left me feeling unsafe? If so, is it possible that it's interfering with my judgment and assessment of danger for myself, my children, or those closest to me?

Do others tell me that I worry too much or tease me about my excessive worry?

Do the things that I worry over rarely come to pass?

If so, am I able to integrate that knowledge or do I quickly move on to the next worry?

If you answer yes to several of those items, your worry is probably interfering with your enjoyment of life and may be interfering with your marriage.

BEGIN TO PUSH BACK AGAINST YOUR WORRIES

Make a conscious decision to push against one or two of the worries that are interfering with your life. Make a commitment to do small steps in the direction of learning to tolerate that worry. The only real antidote, other than medication, is experimenting with new behavior and integrating the knowledge that comes from that behavior.

For example, the treatment for excessive fears, called phobias, is systematic desensitization.[4] In this situation, the fearful person is slowly exposed to the fear-producing stimulus until they learn that it won't produce the effect that they fear. Someone with a phobia of snakes is first asked to think about a snake until they stop feeling anxious. They may first need to be trained to relax, and then do the relaxation techniques at the same time that they see or imagine the fearful stimulus. Once they are able to relax themselves, they then may be shown a picture of a snake, and asked to look at the snake until their anxiety disappears. Next they might watch a movie, then see one in a cage, then one out of a cage, until they are comfortable holding the snake without anxiety. The moral of the example is that the best treatment for excessive anxiety is to move toward it, not away from it, in small graduated steps.

The Worried Husband

While excessive worry is a more common feature among women,[5] many men also have this problem. Mark was raised in a home with parents who constantly worried about money. From a young age, they burdened him with worries about whether they were going to be able to meet the rent, asked Mark for his advice, and overall, treated him as though he had knowledge well past his years. This left Mark feeling worried and preoccupied, much like his parents. From a young age, his parents and others called him Mr. Adult because he had the serious bearing of a much older person. His parents were unable to see that he didn't know how to relax and be playful because they were doing little to give him the opportunity to be a carefree child.

Mark's worried orientation interfered with his ability to relax and enjoy his wife or work. It made him reluctant to take on responsibilities because of a fear that he was going to get it wrong. His laziness wasn't so much a dislike of doing as it was a fear of doing it wrong. When he became a parent, he constantly worried that something bad was going to happen to his family. Early in his marriage, his wife experienced his worry over her and the children as an appealing form of care. However, as the children became older, she began to feel more weighed down by his constant worries and inability to relax and enjoy the many things for which they had to be grateful.

WHAT TO DO IF THIS DESCRIBES YOUR PARTNER

➤ **DON'T CRITICIZE HIM FOR HIS WORRY.** People who worry excessively feel tormented by it and would gladly stop if they could. While you're not his therapist, try to show him that his worries aren't rational. Express this in the form of concern for him such as "It saddens me to see that you feel so tortured by these worries. It's okay with me if you don't do it exactly right."

➤ **TEASE HIM IF HE'LL LET YOU.** People who are worriers often know that they're out of control with it. If he has a sense of humor, try to joke with him about his worries as a way to break the spell that he feels under. This technique only works if he has a sense of humor and he appears to feel relieved by it. Teasing can be humiliating, so stop if it looks as though it's backfiring.

➤ **DON'T ALLOW HIS WORRIES TO RULE THE ROOST.** Worriers can cast a spell on the rest of the household. Watch to make sure this doesn't affect your mood or the mood of the children. You may need to be assertive to make sure that your worrying husband doesn't infect others with his anxieties. If he worries too much in front of the children, show them another option, without undermining him.

People often regulate their behavior in response to their partner's needs, desires, and insecurities, women especially.[6] Therefore be sure to keep doing activities that are meaningful or pleasurable to you, even if your partner refuses out of worry or anxiety.

➤ **HAVE HIM TALK TO HIS DOCTOR ABOUT A MEDICATION EVALUATION**. Excessive worry may be due to a biological condition. There are a number of psychological diagnoses that cause people to worry, such as obsessive-compulsive disorder (OCD), depression, and a host of anxiety disorders. Medications specifically designed to treat anxiety can make a huge difference in someone's ability to relax and enjoy life.[7]

The Perfectionistic Wife

Perfectionists often have a hard time enjoying their lives or their marriages. They constantly hold themselves and others to a standard where the bar is always being raised. Not infrequently, perfectionists come from families where nothing was ever good enough. Their parents were more likely to focus on the B on an otherwise perfect report card. If you're a perfectionist, it may be less the case that you have a lazy husband than that you have unrelenting standards.[8]

Being a perfectionist is stressful because it makes you more likely to believe, often irrationally, that your partner is also holding you to this impossible standard. This is an important perception to gain control over since both men and women feel unhappier in their marriages and communicate less effectively when they expect perfection of themselves.[9] Therefore, if you have perfectionistic expectations of yourself, it's very likely that you're perceiving your partner's communications to you in a negative way.

BARRY: *Vicky is so sensitive to criticism it drives me nuts. If I say, "I want to make sure that we leave the house on time for the party" she hears, "You're always late! Why are you such a flake?!" Or if I have any worries about how the children are doing she reacts like I just accused her of child abuse. I mean, I know she's really hard on herself, but she's twice as hard on me.*

A recent study by Michelle Haring and Paul Hewitt at the University of British Columbia found that wives who had perfectionistic expectations of their husbands had lower marital satisfaction than wives with more moderate expectations.[10] This may be because men's sensitivity to any hint of dominance could cause them to react more negatively to communications about their imperfections. It may also be because people with perfectionistic expectations of themselves or others are less likely to use appreciation, complimenting, affection, and encouragement. They're more likely to use negative approaches such as criticism, contempt, blame, and defensiveness.[11] This style of communication is the least likely to motivate your partner to do more of what you want him to do.[12]

ARE YOU A PERFECTIONIST?

I can't relax if something is incomplete.
Nothing I do is never quite good enough.
I can never stop and take pride in what I've done. I'm
  always off to the next task.
I can never please anyone.

I never can get anything right.

People are always looking for the chink in my armor.

If people get to know me, they'll see how inadequate I really am.

I have to work extremely hard to maintain a good impression and it's really exhausting.

I take pride and pleasure in my hard standards but I drive everyone around me nuts.

Answering yes to several of the above may mean that this something you need to work on.

SOME EXAMPLES OF A PERFECTIONISTIC ORIENTATION TOWARD YOUR SPOUSE ARE:

He can never do things all of the way, it's always half-assed.

If he only tried a little harder, I'd be happier.

I should have married someone more like me and with my standards.

I'm always mad at my husband for one thing or another because he never gets stuff right.

DO YOUR HUSBAND OR OTHERS FREQUENTLY:

➤ say that you're misreading or mishearing what's being said

➤ tell you that you're too sensitive

➤ worry that you don't relax enough

➤ complain that you're overly defensive or overly critical

If these describe you, begin to work on your perfectionism in the following way:

STRIVE TO UNDERSTAND THE ORIGINS OF YOUR FEELINGS

Where did you learn to have these standards? What about your past or your childhood made you feel that something catastrophic would occur if you were less than perfect?

EXAMINE YOUR IRRATIONAL BELIEFS

Go to the section above titled Are You a Perfectionist? Choose three or four of those examples to begin actively working to change them. For example,

People are always looking for the chink in my armor. If I'm not perfect, they won't like me.

Counter: Everyone is imperfect. I deserve to be loved and respected for who I am. If that isn't enough for others, then I'm not going to worry about it.

If people get to know me, they'll see how inadequate I really am.

Counter: I'm just tormenting myself with this belief. I have many great qualities.

I can never stop and take pride in what I've done. I'm always off to the next task.

Counter: Every day I am going to think of at least one good thing that I've done that day or one good thing about myself.

EXAMINE YOUR CRITICISMS ABOUT YOUR HUSBAND

If you're a perfectionist, it's possible that your perfectionism interferes with your ability to see the ways that he positively contributes to the family.[13] It might be worthwhile to make a list of everything that he does for you, the house, and/or the children. Consider whether your marriage might improve if you were to relax your standards in a few of these areas. Pick one or two areas where you'll work to appreciate him, and two other areas where you're going to stop complaining about him.

The Perfectionist Husband

Perfectionists can be hard to live with. Living with a husband who has perfectionistic expectations of you may cause you to feel controlled, dominated, or blamed.[14] You may also feel frustrated that he has a hard time relaxing or feeling good about himself. Overall, men who are perfectionists are less likely to be lazy husbands, since perfectionists tend to be hardworking and obsessive. However, you may be married to a lazy husband who, while not a perfectionist in his own life, has perfectionistic expectations of you.

KATHLEEN: *Craig expects me to do everything exactly like he wants it done. Even though he doesn't do hardly anything around the house or as a parent, he still expects the house to be perfect and for the kids to look like they just walked out of an L.L.Bean catalogue. I feel like, "Hey, you want the kids and the home to look like* House and Garden, *how about you and them pickin' up a broom and start sweeping?"*

Kathleen was right in her observations that Craig had both critical and unrealistic expectations of her. This was a problem because she was already hard on herself in many ways. As a result, when Craig was critical, she retaliated with hostility. This cycle of criticism and countercriticism around perfectionistic standards caused a lot of unhappiness between them.

Women who feel they have to be perfect are more likely to feel anxious, guilty, or depressed.[15] Therefore, if you live with a perfectionist husband, it's important to gain some immunity to how his standards make you feel. Bearing this in mind, consider the following questions. I react to my husband's perfectionism by:

feeling that I have to be respond quickly
worrying all the time that I'm disappointing him
doing more than I want to in order to avoid his complaining
feeling anxious, self-critical, or depressed

If your partner's perfectionism causes you to behave in ways that aren't good for you, it may mean that you haven't fully understood how your past affects the present. For example:

Why do you feel obligated to change your behavior to meet your husband's standards?
Why do you feel so worried about disappointing or upsetting him?

What's the worst that can happen if you don't live up to his standards?

If you feel intimidated by your husband, the guidelines set forth in the next section on living with an angry husband will provide guidance about how to begin to counter his effect on you.

The Angry Husband

Living with a hostile or abusive spouse can make you feel depressed, inadequate, anxious, or afraid.[16] If your partner is frequently hostile, his laziness may be the least of your worries. You may first need to learn how to decrease his hold over you before you can effectively strategize how to get him to do more with the house and kids.

An angry husband may treat you in a controlling, belittling, or domineering way. He may use his size, loudness, or tone of voice to intimidate you. He may be extremely jealous and make you accountable to him in ways that are neither fair nor reasonable. His behavior may extend to restricting your time with friends or family members. He may use intimidation to get you to be sexual when you don't want to be.[17]

The following strategies are suggested if your partner is verbally domineering or verbally abusive. If he is physically abusive, that may require a different set of strategies, one that is beyond the scope of this book. If your husband is physically abusive, see resources listed at endnotes for this chapter.[18] One of the first steps to dealing with your partner's hostility is to deeply understand how it's affecting your mood and behavior. For example, consider the following questions. As a result of my partner's hostility, I:

> ➤ frequently don't go to places or see people that I want to see
> ➤ do much more for him, the house, or the children than is fair or reasonable
> ➤ constantly worry that my behavior is going to get me yelled at

If any of these are true, you should begin developing a plan to liberate yourself from his hold on you before considering how to get him to do more. This is because you can't negotiate for change from a position of fear or intimidation.

JANE: *Randy makes me feel like I'm the laziest, most selfish person in the world if I just ask him to clear the table or help get the kids to bed. He'll start screaming at the top of his lungs. It's really, really obnoxious. I just end up not asking him to do anything because he makes me feel so awful about myself.*

Jane's decision to stop making demands is a common one for women where men use their anger as a way to get out of work and avoid activities that they don't want to do. The first thing you have to assess is whether you're truly in any physical danger if you don't act or behave in the way that your husband wants you to. While there is no foolproof guarantee that some-one won't escalate their verbal abuse into physical abuse, the following checklist may provide some guidance. Consider the following:

> Has your partner ever struck you?
> Did he ever hit a woman in his prior marriage or relationship?
> Has he been in physical altercations with others as an adult?
> Does he have a history of impulsive and/or antisocial behavior?
> Has he ever threatened to hit you?

Answering yes to one or more of the above may indicate that you're at risk for physical abuse from your husband. This is an important distinction because people who have a history of battering are more likely to do so when their wives become more strong or separate in the ways that I'm going to encourage you to become.[19] If you don't believe that you're at risk for battering, then my job is to help you understand why you feel so intimidated by your husband and help you to become more self-interested and assertive.

There are many reasons why women end up complying with their husband's anger. Some common examples are as follows:

> It makes me feel terrible about myself when he gets mad at me.
> I don't want the children to witness conflict.
> It's not worth it to me to see him so upset, so I just give in.
> I feel sorry for him.

Let's examine these.

IT MAKES ME FEEL TERRIBLE ABOUT MYSELF
WHEN HE GETS MAD AT ME

One of the challenges of marriage is to gain control over how much the other's behavior affects how we feel about ourselves.[20] In general, people who have been abused or criticized in their childhoods are more vulnerable to being intimidated and controlled in their marriages. This is because they developed irrational beliefs about themselves and others in response to their abuse. Children who grow up in abusive or neglectful homes develop beliefs that they're not entitled to protect themselves from mistreatment. In some cases, they may not even be able to *tell* what is mistreatment.[21]

> **GINA**: *My father was an alcoholic and had a really bad temper. He's definitely what they call a mean drunk and he was drunk most of the time. I don't even like to think about half the things he called me, let alone say them out loud. And he wasn't shy about using the belt either. But we didn't know any different growing up. It wasn't until I was in therapy that I even began to learn how bad it was.*

Gina entered individual therapy because of feelings of depression and anxiety. As we began talking, it became clear that she was tolerating a lot of verbal abuse from her husband and that her depression and anxiety were tied to her marriage. Gina didn't feel in any danger physically from her husband and had no desire to leave him. However, she didn't know what to do to get him to change.

The first step for Gina was learning how her past was affecting her view of the present. Because there was no indication that she was in any physical danger from Greg, I encouraged her to consider how she would need to change in order to become less intimidated by him. We began by looking at the beliefs that she had developed from her childhood. I had Gina keep a journal for two weeks as a way to begin identifying her beliefs. In the journal, she wrote down her response to every interaction that generated an emotion, and wrote down the accompanying belief. This kind of exercise is useful in helping you become more conscious of how you to talk to yourself.[22] Her journal looked like this:

> MONDAY: Greg blew up at me when I asked him if he could come home early instead of going to the gym in order to help me with the kids' school science project.
> EMOTION: fear, anger
> BELIEF: He's a jerk, but maybe I'm being selfish to want him to help me with the kids since he works so hard.

> WEDNESDAY: Greg lost it because I was an hour late getting ready to have dinner with his parents.
> EMOTION: fear, guilt
> BELIEF: I'm such a flake sometimes.

As Gina and I examined her journal, the following irrational beliefs emerged:

Irrational Beliefs
I deserve to be shamed, criticized, or humiliated.
Others' needs are more important than mine.

Women should submit to a man's authority.

I don't deserve protection.

If someone's mad at me, I better get away as fast as possible.

These irrational beliefs had the effect of keeping Gina cowed and compliant in her marriage. In order to help her gain control over these beliefs, she needed to directly confront them. To do this, we used cognitive-behavioral techniques.[23] For example, a part of her worksheet looked like this:

Irrational Belief:

I deserve to be shamed, criticized, or humiliated.

Emotional response to the belief

Fear, guilt, shame, anxiety

Behavioral response:

Withdrawal, compliance

Positive counterstatement:

I deserve to be spoken to with respect and kindness.

Behavioral response:

1. Tell Greg that I didn't like how he spoke to me.
2. Next time he yells at me, calmly tell him to lower his voice. If he refuses, tell him that if he can't speak to me in a more respectful way, I'm going to leave the room.

STATE YOUR REQUESTS WITH AN ASSUMPTION OF COOPERATION

GINA: I need more help with the house and kids and am wondering what you'd be willing to start doing.

GREG: I told you, I already work hard at my job and when I come home I don't have the time or energy to do one more thing.

GINA: I understand that. I know your job is exhausting, but so is raising children, making meals, and keeping the house clean. My job's really tiring too.

GREG: (raising voice) Look, why do you have to bug me about this stuff? The last thing I want to do when I come home is change diapers and do laundry. Is that so hard for you to understand?

GINA: Greg, don't raise your voice with me. I'm making a reasonable request that you not dump everything to do with the house and kids on me. It's not like I'm a stay-at-home mom, I also work outside the home.

GREG: Part-time at this easy job, how hard is that!

GINA: I'm not discussing with you whether my job is easy or hard. The point is that I bring in income to the family too and currently do everything and it's not fair. I need you to do more.

GREG: (shouting) I told you, I'm not doing any damned housework so you can just forget about it!

This conversation could go many ways, most of them unproductive for the first few times. Bearing this in mind, she should present Greg with a list of things that he could do and ask him to choose some later that day, or the next. Her tone of voice when she presents the list should be affectionate and upbeat. There should be an assumption of cooperation and a belief that he wants to make her happy. The easier the tasks, the greater number he should choose—the harder, the fewer number of tasks. She might find it useful to have a "hard" column and an "easy" column, and ask him to choose several from each.

DON'T LET YOUR INTIMIDATION RULE YOU

Gina will need to stay in the game with Greg if he's been able to intimidate her in the past. People change slowly, and he may not do anything differently until he's clear that the old tactics no longer work.[24] Therefore, while she shouldn't let these interactions deteriorate into a nasty fight, she should keep up this discussion at least once a week. In fact, if he has always been able to shut her down with his attitude, it would be better for her to let the discussion escalate into a fight to show him that she's changing the rules rather than back down at the first sign of trouble. It's possible that she will feel or become verbally aggressive at first because most people have a hard time making a smooth transition from being intimidated to assertive. Typically, they swing all the way over to aggressive and then have to learn how to rein it back down by practicing over time.

I'm not advocating that you start out aggressively, because, overall, aggression in negotiations is counterproductive (though it's working for Greg and many other men like a charm). Rather, I'm saying that you shouldn't be too surprised or too worried if that happens. The main idea is to commit to a new form of behavior for a set period of time, such as the next six months to a year, assume there will be ups and downs, and keep your eyes on the prize.

Gina's most serious obstacle isn't just Greg, it's also her anxiety and lack of entitlement. If this describes you, you'll have to fake it till you make it for a while. Acting in an entitled way may feel foreign if not outright phony. It may bring up significant anxiety, guilt, even shame. That's why you should plan on a six-month-to-a-year campaign of working on this issue.

I DON'T WANT THE CHILDREN TO WITNESS CONFLICT

Another common reason why women submit to their husband's dominance is a fear of a harmful and escalating fight. Many parents worry that any marital fight is potentially traumatizing to their children. While children clearly prefer it if their parents never fight, children are generally not harmed by parental fights provided that:

> the fights typically resolve
> the children aren't blamed for the conflict
> the marriage isn't characterized by chaos, out-of-control verbal and/or physical abuse, or ongoing shame or humiliation[25]

As I noted earlier, some of the happiest marriages are those where the couples fight. However, for every fight, these couples have at least five positive exchanges afterward.[26] I highlight this because if you're trying to protect your children from fighting by caving in to your husband, you may not be doing yourself, your children, or your marriage any favor. It may be better for you to get strong enough to stand up to him. In addition, he may respect you more if you do.[27] People who are bullies rarely respect those whom they bully. They know at some level that they're out of control, and may unconsciously want you to rein them in.[28]

This doesn't mean that he will make it easy on you. If the pattern has persisted for a while, it won't change overnight. But, getting an angry husband to start behaving begins with your getting strong enough to insist on his treating you better.

IT'S NOT WORTH IT TO ME TO SEE HIM SO UPSET, SO I JUST GIVE IN

This statement is often made from a place of low self-esteem and a low sense of entitlement. While we all have to pick and choose our battles in marriage, living with a hostile spouse means learning how to deal with your husband's upset without freaking out about it. People who are overly responsible for others have a hard time with this one. That's because they were raised to believe that others' needs are more important than theirs. They have an inadequate reserve of strength to draw on when they want to go up against someone who so clearly wants to get his way. This is another one of those places where women's socialization to be other-focused compromises them in their dealings with a man's out-of-control sense of entitlement.

If this characterizes you, strive to understand where your lack of entitlement came from. Write a letter to the people who hurt you or made you feel that you don't deserve to be treated well. You can decide later whether or not to mail it. Make a list of all of the behaviors you tolerate that you wish you didn't. For example, Gina made the following list of behaviors that she wanted to change:

I allow myself to be yelled at and disrespected.
I don't ask enough for help and participation from my husband and kids.
I don't do enough to nurture myself because I always put myself last.
I let others define how I should think of myself.
I let guilt rule my life.

I FEEL SORRY FOR HIM

In this scenario, your feelings of overresponsibility directly interfere with your ability to put forth your agenda. Many women can see that underneath their husband's bluster is a scared boy. While this awareness can contribute to a useful degree of compassion, it may compromise these wives if they're trying too hard to prop up their husbands. For example, women who grew up with fathers who are weak, fragile, or dependent may feel so worried about hurting a man's feelings that they never appropriately challenge them.

> **WINNIE**: *My father struggled with depression throughout all of my childhood and my mom was a real bitch to him about it. She'd tell him he wasn't a "real man" or talk about how lucky so-and-so was because her husband was such a big, strong, man. I used to want to slug her because you could just see him shrink down whenever she'd yell at him.*

Winnie was unable to use her strength in her marriage because she associated it with being destructive. She grew up feeling so saddened by her father's lack of strength that she wanted to make sure she never made a man feel the way mother had made her father feel. She was attracted to her husband, in part, because he was clearly much stronger than her dad. While she felt relieved that her husband was able to demand what he wanted in marriage, she nonetheless worried that he'd crumble the way her father did with her mother if she stood up to him. As a result, she wrote him a blank check about how little he had to do with the house or children. Winnie needed to learn that her husband could tolerate her standing up to him before she could start making the kinds of demands she needed to make.

IF YOU FEEL AFRAID OF YOUR STRENGTH CONSIDER THE FOLLOWING:

Examine where your beliefs come from. They were probably developed in childhood and therefore may no longer be relevant.

Work to see that it's not your job to hold up your husband. A marriage is made strong by two equals. You don't benefit him or yourself if you restrict your power too much.

Examine your sense of guilt. If he complains that you're too hurtful, strive to see if your communication really is problematic or if this is just a manipulation by him to get you off his back.

GOING FORWARD WITH THE ANGRY HUSBAND

You should begin to make the changes I'm recommending right away. People who live with an intimidating spouse often believe that it's going to get better someday. The opposite is true. If you wait until you feel completely comfortable or safe, nothing will change. Standing up to an intimidating man takes courage, but it can mean the difference between a good marriage and a marriage that's more like a form of slavery.

In addition, letting yourself be intimidated by your husband isn't great role modeling for your children. Children benefit from seeing both of their parents strive to have their needs met, without being too selfish or too selfless. If you're married to an angry husband, you may well be settling for too little in the marriage. If changing in the ways that I'm recommending seems too daunting, get help and support from a therapist. But start today.

The Angry Wife

While some women respond to childhood abuse by becoming passive and intimidated, others become combative and argumentative. This is done as a way to never again feel vulnerable. Unfortunately, these women approach every interaction with guns blazing, and as a result are more likely to make their husbands feel belittled, resentful, and resistant to change.

> BONNIE: *Ned says I'm too hard on him, but frankly, he deserves it. I do everything and he sits on his lazy ass and asks for more. He says it's bad for the kids for me to always be cussing him out in front of them, but, hey, if he doesn't like it, he can either get the hell out or get off his butt and give me a hand.*

Bonnie brought a lot of hurt and anger into her marriage from her childhood. As a result, she believes that if she lets her guard down, people will take advantage of her. This siege mentality causes her to be suspicious and cynical in her dealings with her husband and often her children and friends. She gets offended easily and quickly goes on the attack when she senses potential conflict. This is a common lesson learned from a conflict-ridden childhood—"better to hurt them than to let them hurt you." However, it's outgrown its usefulness. She has a right to be annoyed at Ned if he's uninvolved with the house and kids, but her style decreases the likelihood that he'll want to change.

Growing up with parents who were critical, depressed, or neglectful could have created this problem for you. It may have left you feeling excessively entitled to be treated well. You may have concluded that you never wanted to be deprived again, and this may cause you to be hostile, defensive, or vigilant to any hint that your needs won't be met. You may approach negotiations assuming the worst rather than assuming mutuality and cooperation. If this is the case, your husband's "laziness" may be an attempt to guard against feeling excessively controlled, belittled, or hurt by you. Once again, people don't change with a gun to their heads, at least not for long. The most effective and lasting change occurs when people want to make each other happy.

Studies show that people in distressed marriages underestimate how much their partner is doing by as much as 50 percent![29] When I saw Bonnie and Ned in couple's therapy, it became clear that Bonnie was denying how much Ned *was* contributing to the house and kids. While Bonnie was telling herself and Ned that she was being neglected, even mistreated by him, over time it became obvious that she was wrong in her assessments. Her fears of being vulnerable caused her to constantly amp up her complaints against Ned as a way to keep her defenses primed and vigilant. In other words, she felt safer hating Ned than loving him. As we got more into the therapy, I began to see how terrified Bonnie was of being vulnerable. In order to gain a more realistic view of Ned, she needed to be willing to approach him in a more conciliatory fashion and not see this as begging. People who have been shamed or humiliated in childhood sometimes feel that a more modulated approach is equivalent to submission. They need to learn that you can be both kind and self-protective at the same time.

Consider the following:

Do people other than your husband accuse you of being critical?

Do you sometimes offend people and not know why?

Do your kids often complain or act as if you hurt their feelings?

Do you have a hard time maintaining relationships with friends or coworkers?

Has your anger gotten you into trouble at work or in relations with family or friends?

If you answer yes to more than one of the above questions, it may mean that your past has too great an influence on the present. You may need additional help such as psychotherapy to help you gain control over those painful feelings.

DEALING WITH GUILT

Angry behavior can create intense feelings of guilt. Unfortunately, guilt about past behavior increases the likelihood that the behavior will occur again. This is because guilt contributes to feelings of self-hatred and nothing good ever comes of that. Self-hatred makes the world a scarier place because it produces the fear that others will "discover" the things in you that you hate about yourself. Self-hatred reduces your resilience because so many of your internal resources go to proving the other wrong in your mind. You may also spend too much time reducing others' capacity to make you feel bad by devaluing them, or keeping people so intimidated or bewildered that they never want to get close enough to affect you.

Moving toward self-forgiveness and self-compassion increases your resilience. This is because those qualities make you less oriented toward other people's reactions. They give you control over how you're going to feel about yourself because *you* claim the right to decide how you get to feel about yourself.

EXERCISE ON GUILT

List some behaviors that you feel chronically guilty about. Some common examples are:

> I feel guilty about losing my patience with my children and/or my husband.
>
> I feel guilty that I don't spend enough time with my children/husband/friends/parents.
>
> I feel bad about yelling at my husband or kids in the same way that I was yelled at when I was a kid.
>
> I feel guilty about hitting my kids or husband.
>
> I feel guilty that I don't do more with or for my parents.

PLEDGE

I want you to seriously commit to a program of forgiving yourself for whatever you currently accuse yourself of doing or not doing. Many people resist this commitment, because they believe that they're letting themselves off too easily. If you're worried that you're letting yourself off too easily, you probably aren't. People who let themselves off too easily aren't yet at the place where they're consciously thinking about the impact of their behavior on others. Again, the shortest path to decreasing behavior that you don't like in yourself is moving toward self-forgiveness, self-compassion, and a commitment to change.

Below are some positive self-statements to combat guilt and shame. If guilt is a serious problem for you, write these statements out on a three-by-five-inch card and carry them with you. Read them once in the morning and once before you go to bed.

I am deserving of love and forgiveness.

Self-hatred is bad for me and for my family.

It's not my fault that terrible things happened to me in my life.

I am a good person, even if I've upset or disappointed those closest to me.

I am deserving of compassion, even if I've done things that have been hurtful to others. I'm working to repair whatever hurt I've caused.

Anaïs Nin wrote, "We don't see things as they are. We see them how *we* are." Our personalities and our pasts are filters that constantly color our experience. They let in information and they keep information out. This can be useful in alerting us to danger, however it can also distort our perceptions of our partners and children, and alert us to dangers where none exist. Our gender is another of these filters. In the next chapter, we'll look at the male gender and see how men view the world, and why you may be having such a hard time understanding them.

· 7 ·

What's with Men, Anyway?

A book titled *Everything Men Know About Women*, created by Cindy Cashman, has sold more than a million copies. The book is filled with blank pages.[1] I regularly hear my women clients complain about the supposedly clueless and selfish nature of the male. "What's with your gender? How come they don't get it? How come guys are so useless with feelings? Why don't men communicate better? Why does he try to fix me when I want him to just listen? Why is everything up to me?"

This chapter will take a hard look at these common questions and find out what's going on inside the sometimes perplexing world of the guy. We will peer through a variety of these lenses as a way to increase your ability to gain more involvement from him, and more peace in your household. We'll see how jobs cause men to prioritize their careers over their families, how men's childhoods affect their view of themselves, and how the ever-shifting definition of what it means to be a man affects their well-being and behavior. We'll look at how men communicate, and what may need to change in you or your home in order to get your partner to do more of his fair share. Finally, we'll look at how biological and cultural differences shape men's perspective and behavior.

Status Seekers

If men appear more self-centered than women, it may be because they live in a world where their status determines the quality of the women they attract, the amount of income they earn, and the amount of respect that they command in other men's eyes. While this may be slowly changing, the reality is that most people define a man's success in economic and social terms more than in their abilities as a husband or father.[2] A mediocre dad and husband who's a millionaire will command a lot more respect from other men than a great father and husband who doesn't earn very much.

This reality is most visible in the workplace. Very few employers are sympathetic to men's desires to put their families first. In the same way that career women are taken off the fast track when they reduce their workload in order to spend more time with their children,[3] men are also penalized when they prioritize their families. While most men state that they value their families over their jobs, the majority of them are unable or unwilling to put these priorities into practice.[4] For example, Ann Crittenden notes that Houston Oiler David Williams was docked $111,111 when he missed a game to attend the birth of his infant.[5] In companies with over one hundred workers, only 1 percent are offered paid paternity leave and only 18 percent receive unpaid paternity leaves.[6] In those cases where men are offered these benefits, few take advantage of them for fear of being stigmatized, and because of the potential long-term consequences for their careers and finances.

The double bind of these realities cause many men to feel resentful and confused when their wives complain about how preoccupied they are with work.

> **MANUEL**: *Rosie's always saying that it's selfish of me to spend so much time at work and not that much with her and the kids. Unfortunately, if she wants to have her new kitchen or a vacation or her new car, then it means that I need to work all of the time. I miss spending time with my children too, but I'm trying to give my family some of the opportunities that neither one of us ever had.*

Men also worry that spending time at home instead of work decreases their status with other men who are busy earning and enlarging their income or careers. They worry that they're less admirable as men if they don't have the spoils of status that a career or income can bring. Men can feel unworthy and inadequate if they don't have the big-game prizes that other men use to demonstrate their worth.[7] This may be one of the reasons that in poorer neighborhoods, disrespecting another man's reputation is a common ground for assault or murder. Not having material goods to demonstrate one's value, they are left with their reputation and honor.[8]

Empathy

Empathy is the ability to sense or feel what others are thinking and feeling, and men may come by it a little less easily than women.[9] This also causes men to look self-centered from a woman's perspective. Studies show that young girls show superiority over boys in their ability to read facial expressions, read tone of voice, judge a person's character, and understand another's thoughts and intentions by the age of three.[10] Girls also show more interest in being fair, taking turns,[11] and demonstrating a desire to comfort others in distress from a young age.[12] As adults, women's conversations involve more discussion of feelings and relationships, which is key to empathy (and guilt), while men's conversations focus more on exchange of information.[13]

This difference is also seen in how the two genders manage conflict in a family. In one study of families, mothers made far more concessions during family conflicts than fathers or sons.[14] Girls growing up in this environment would conclude that if there's conflict, women are supposed to concede. This environment could also lead women to believe that men's needs are more important.

Clearly, some of these gender differences may stem from socialization. For example, parents use the language of emotion far more frequently with their daughters than their sons. Fathers are more likely to issue commands to children, and more commands to their sons than their daughters.[15] Moms tend to use more emotion words with their toddler daughters than their sons, and also to use more words of positive emotion. While boys are supported in being aggressive or assertive by their peer groups and parents, girls are more frequently censored by both groups for this behavior.[16] The phrase "boys will be boys" constitutes a wink of the eye to rowdy mischief and rule breaking, while girls are rarely afforded the same acceptance at home or on the playground. In other words, from very early on, girls are socialized toward being aware of and sensitive to the feelings of others while boys are less frequently socialized in this direction. Therefore, females who "behave insensitively" are far more likely to feel guilt (self-condemnation) than a boy, who doesn't have that standard of behavior.

Women's traditional financial dependence on men may have also made them better at being able to read another's feelings because it was in their best interest to do so. That is, it pays for those with less power to be more responsive and sensitive to those with more power.[17]

Biology

The way in which biology affects behavioral differences between the sexes is a source of intense interest, research, and debate. Because biological explanations of gender have historically been used to further women's oppression, it's important that these differences be examined critically. Psychologist Steven Pinker, before summarizing some of this research in his book *The Blank Slate,* offers this preface: "Men and women have all the same genes except for a handful on the Y-chromosome, and their brains are so similar that it takes an eagle-eyed neuroanatomist to find the small difference between them. Their average levels of general intelligence are the same, according to the best psychometric estimates, and they use language and think about the physical and living world in the same general way. They feel the same basic emotions, and both enjoy sex, seek intelligent and kind marriage partners, get jealous, make sacrifices for their children, compete for status and mates, and sometimes commit aggression in pursuit of their interests. But of course, the minds of men and women aren't identical, and recent reviews of sex differences have converged on some reliable differences."

Let's look at some of these differences in women's versus men's attitudes toward parenting. For example, women's comparative preoccupation with their children may have to do with evolutionary differences in how many times women get to reproduce over the course of their lifetimes.[18] While men can produce a potential offspring every time they have sex, women only generate an average of one egg a month and a finite number of ova over a limited number of years. Evolutionary psychologists believe that these differences in reproductive opportunity and strategy affect each gender's approach to sex, reproduction, parenting, and long-term relationships.[19]

From an evolutionary perspective, women may be more worried about and preoccupied with their children's well-being than men because they have fewer chances to pass on their genes. While a man's contribution to creating and often caring for a child is a simple donation of sperm, a woman has to carry the child for nine months, and in almost every culture has primary responsibility for its survival. As anthropologist Sarah Hrdy writes, "Like it or not, each of us lives with the emotional legacy and decision-making equipment of mothers who acted so as to ensure that at least one offspring survived to reproduce. . . ." She cites authors such as Jane Austen and Edith Wharton, whose female protagonists worked hard to make sure that their children made it up the social ladder. "We tend to think of these mothers as 'controlling,' 'pushy,' 'interfering'—and I don't disagree—but the venerable ancestry of such traits is worth considering."[20]

Are Men Wired to Care Less About Parenting Than Women?

Cross-culture studies reveal that when households are female headed, the nutritional needs of children are much better provided for than in father-headed households. Crittenden reports that in Kenya and Malawi, the more that men controlled the family's financial resources among sugarcane farmers, the less money was spent on food for the rest of the family. This was because men were more likely than women to spend money on alcohol. The same finding was made in Jamaica.[21] In Brazil, one dollar in the hands of a mother is the equivalent of eighteen dollars in the hands of a father in terms of a child's survival rate. Similar findings have been made in Guatemala, South India, the Ivory Coast, and Ghana.[22] In fact, these results have been shown so consistently across cultures that many countries have created policies to reduce poverty by granting funds directly to mothers rather than fathers.

Anthropologists believe that men's lower investment in their children over other activities could have ancient roots related to establishing paternity. Hrdy argues that throughout evolution, women could be confident that investing all of their energies in their children increased their reproductive success; after all, women *know* that the child they deliver is theirs. Therefore, a man's decision to be very involved with the children may mean that he's contributing to the survival of somebody else's genes instead of his own. For these reasons, nature may have set the threshold of involvement slightly higher for fathers than it did for mothers,[23] the so-called "mom's babies—dad's maybes" idea.

The Aka pygmies of central Africa are evidence of this, too. In Aka society, wives spend an unusual amount of time by their husband's side and, as a result, the husband is far more involved as a parent. One explanation is that an Aka man has a great deal of certainty that he is the father of his children because of the small amount of time the mother has for philandering.[24] This is far less the case in cultures such as the Huikuru of Amazonia where it's not uncommon for men and women to have as many as four to twelve lovers at a time.[25] In those cultures, men would be right to worry that the children that were carried by his wife might have been sired by one of her many lovers.

So if men bring slightly less investment into the parental picture, what causes them to be more involved? Women, apparently. In those cultures where women have more status, men are much more significantly involved.[26] The Father's Commission in Sweden found that the more fulfilled and economically successful the mother, the more likely she was to enlist the father's help, and to create the space for his involvement.[27] A recent paper published by the Council on Contemporary Families shows that men in the United States do more housework than men in France, Germany, Italy, or Japan. This is probably because women in the United States have more social and financial power to get men to be more involved. The exception to this was Sweden, where men do an average of eight more hours of housework a week than American men and social policies support egalitarian parenting.[28]

Okay, this is all well and good and interesting, and thanks for all the info on anthropology and evolution, and I'll be sure to consult you the next time I find a fossil or an Aka tribesman in my backyard, but what am I supposed to do with it? Well, let's start with communication. In 1990, sociolinguist Deborah Tannen published her now classic book on the differences in the sexes titled *You Just Don't Understand.* The book argues that many misunderstandings between men and women occur because women's communication is more commonly oriented toward intimacy, consensus building, and cooperation, while men's communication is oriented around preserving feelings of independence, autonomy, and status. While there are always huge exceptions in any statement about gender, many studies have shown her views to have validity.[29] In the following section, we'll look at some of these differences and examine how understanding them can be used to develop a strategy for change in your household.

Don't Tell Me What to Do

Women often observe that men resent any suggestion that they're obeying a wife's orders. As a husband said to me recently, "I don't want to feel like I have to hop to it as soon as she asks me to do something. I'll get to it, I just want to get to it in my own time." Why would men be so sensitive to something as simple as a request? Here again it may relate to men's vulnerability to any hint of subordinance. Doing something because they're told to suggests that they have low status. Refusing to do the task, however trivial, asserts their independence.

This sensitivity to status is another area of confusion because women are more likely to see relationships in an interdependent way, where making requests of the other is part of the give-and-take of a relationship. As Tannen writes, "Women's lives have historically been hemmed in at every turn by the demands of others—their families, their husbands—and yet, though individual women may complain of overbearing husbands, there is no parallel stereotype of a roosterpecked wife. Why not? Seeing people as interdependent, women expect their actions to be influenced by others and they expect people to act in concert."[30]

Many researchers have found that men's sensitivity to differences in status start early and are reflected in the ways that boys and girls play. For example, boys spend more time than girls monitoring who's on top and who's on the bottom of a social hierarchy at the playground.[31] They are also more likely to score higher on themes related to power and control on psychological tests such as the Friendship and Relationship Questionnaire while girls rank friendship and intimacy higher.[32] Girls are far more likely to communicate in ways that take others into consideration such as "Let's play with this," "How about if we? . . . ," etc. When boys play, they more commonly use language of dominance and aggression, highlighting a style that is less oriented to how the other is feeling and more to asserting their position or authority. They are more likely to issue orders such as, "Give me that. Get out of here. That's mine!"[33]

Males' preoccupation with status and power often appear early in their fantasy lives. When children are invited to make up stories, boys typically write about their accomplishments and strengths. In these tales, the boys are heroes, saviors, and conquerors. Girls more often write stories that involve others, and less commonly highlight themselves as heroes or victors.[34] These gender differences often carry into adulthood. Men in the United States and Western Europe are more likely to see themselves as having talents or strengths that others don't possess, even when this isn't true. Goethals referred to this as the "false uniqueness bias" in men.[35] Women are less likely to have this orientation.

Of course, none of this is to say that girls can't be aggressive or competitive. However, girls and women are more likely to demonstrate these feelings and behaviors through social exclusion, innuendo, and gossip than through physical displays and aggressive verbal domineering.[36]

Communicating in Marriage

Women often feel disadvantaged in conversations with men because women expect more reciprocity and consideration in their listeners. Women are more likely to think, *I've let you speak and asked you about yourself, now I'd like to speak and you should ask me about myself.* And in woman-to-woman conversations, this is more commonly how it goes.

This is far less the case in woman-to-man conversations, where men are more likely to dominate a conversation (at least in public or when they're dating. Once men are involved and at home, they are more likely to be quiet).[37] In either case, it isn't so much that men don't care about what women have to say (I believe that they do). It's more that they assume if a woman has something to say, she'll butt in with challenges, opinions, and objections, in the same way that he would. While this isn't always true, sometimes a man's inclination to challenge, interrupt, or proclaim is a demonstration of respect rather than an attempt to be domineering or controlling.[38] However, because women are less likely to communicate in this way, and more likely to be censored by others when they do, confusion and conflict often occur.[39]

LISTENING

Men can sometimes appear more self-involved than women because of the way that they listen (or don't, depending on your perspective). Women use much more eye contact when they're in conversation, ask more questions, and offer more encouragement such as smiling, laughing, and agreeing.[40] As a rule, men don't tend to ask as many questions or make as many soothing or reassuring sounds when they're engaged in conversation. They're also more likely to give advice, make statements, and challenge rather than ask questions or agree.[41] Women commonly will greet another with a compliment ("Great shirt," "I love your earrings," "Where did you get those shoes?") whereas this behavior is rare with men.

Men sometimes appear more self-centered in conversation because they can experience the act of listening at length as subordinance. Giving advice, challenging, or making suggestions allows men to feel like they're in a position of equality, if not superiority. Here too, I would argue that men *do* listen, they just do so in a different way and for different themes.

However, males of all ages appear to use far less eye contact than females, in general. In fact, newborn boys engage in a lot less eye contact than newborn girls. This finding has been tied to testosterone levels; the higher the level of testosterone, the less eye contact shown for both boys and girls. Young boys, teens, and young men are far more likely to avoid eye contact, and to sit parallel to another person rather than face-to-face.[42] In conversation, this can leave their frustrated female listeners feeling hurt, ignored, or unimportant.

ASKING FOR HELP

Sex differences also surface around the issue of self-disclosure and seeking help. For example, men are far less likely to disclose emotions for fear that they'll be shamed or humiliated in the process. From his vantage point, asking for help creates vulnerability to others' feeling superior or behaving in a superior way. The classic example of men refusing to ask for directions is evidence of this dynamic.

And men *are* sometimes shamed when they ask for help or appear weak. A study of college students found that male dorm students were far more rejecting of a roommate's depressed behavior than were women with a depressed female roommate. Women, on the other hand often connect through the disclosure of vulnerabilities.[43]

One of the common times that men and women misunderstand each other is when a woman wants to be understood and a man responds with advice. From the man's perspective, he believes that he can most effectively demonstrate his concern and talents through problem solving. For his wife, his solving the problem may suggest that she was too stupid to figure it out herself. Ironically, as I frequently observe in my practice, women's rejection of men's advice or help can leave men feeling hurt, belittled, or insignificant.

RANK, HOUSEWORK, AND PARENTING

A concern about looking weak is sometimes at the heart of men's resistance to parenting or housework. This is one of the ways that both men and women suffer from our culture's devaluing of family work. From this perspective, your husband may stonewall, make excuses, avoid, and evade family work in order to prove to you that he has status as a man, odd as that may seem, more than because he really believes that you have no right to ask. Some men believe that their wives won't respect them as much if they *do* more housework and parenting. This belief is reinforced in traditional or transitional homes where women sometimes resist men's help.[44] I'm not saying, so just understand him and forget about his doing his share. I'm saying that understanding him is a first step to getting him to change.

ASK, DON'T TELL

Because men are sensitive to any suggestion that they are of lower status, you will probably get more cooperation if you state your requests as requests and not demands. I know, I know. He has no problems telling you to do things and you don't get all huffy on him—or maybe you do and that's part of the problem. Either way, asking is almost always a better strategy.

> PHILLIP: *I have an allergic reaction to any request Suzie makes that begins with, "You need to . . ." "You need to empty the dishwasher, you need to clean out the kitty litter, you need to get the mail out of the mailbox more frequently." I always feel like, "I don't need to do jack." If she wants me*

to do something, she should just ask me rather than tell me it's something I need to do.

When women "nag" they do so assuming that if their husbands really heard and understood their concerns, they would do what they requested. Again, women's interdependent orientation may leave them confused when men don't respond in kind.[45] For men, doing activities in their own time frame promotes a feeling that they're doing it "because they want to not because they have to."[46]

> **ARTHUR:** *I hate it when we have company over and Cathy starts giving me a bunch of directions. I just feel like it makes me look like I'm a wimp or someone who's being run around by his wife.*

NEGOTIATE STANDARDS

As we saw earlier, differences in standards are a common place where couples have problems. This is especially true in the realm of parenting. Fathers sometimes parent in ways that are quite different from mothers. For example, fathers are less likely to spend as much time talking or inquiring about feelings with their children. Their interactions with children are often oriented toward excitement and stimulation, and children frequently look to fathers to provide this. This appears to be something that exists across cultures and highlights the fact that while fathers care, they appear to care in a different way.[47]

However, these parenting differences can cause problems at

home. A common complaint from mothers is, "His idea of spending time with the children is letting them crawl around the floor underneath his feet while he reads the paper or watches TV. I don't call that quality time." Well, hold on there. Children don't require active, minute-to-minute interaction in order to grow and develop. Kids learn a lot from crawling around on the floor at dad's feet, even if he isn't actively involved with them. It's a way to feel independent knowing that a parent is standing by, if needed.

Of course this isn't all they need. Children also want parents who are tuned in to their moods and needs; if dad is conked out on the couch while his one-year-old is exploring the many things that can be neatly inserted into a light socket, that's a different story. In addition, if dad doesn't spend *any* time with the children, they'll feel neglected and neither will feel close to the other later in life. However, women commonly experience men as being uninterested or uninvolved when they're simply being involved in a different way. They spoil a potentially good relationship between father and child by being too danged worried.

For example, Scott and Mary are new parents of a four-month-old girl. Mary worries that Scott will be insensitive to their daughter, even though he's never done anything to prove that. As a result, she hovers when Scott has the baby and offers endless suggestions about how she should be changed, fed, burped, carried, and put down for a nap. It's well-meaning and she does know more about babies having been the eldest child in a family of seven kids. However, she's blowing it with Scott by not paying attention to how her behavior makes him feel.

Mary needs to accept that Scott will have different standards for parenting. This may mean that she'll have to leave Scott alone with the baby so that they can get to know each other, attach to each other, and so Scott can learn how the whole baby thing works. Doing this will not only increase the amount of time he'll want to spend with the baby, it will make him like Mary more. It may even make him more motivated to do housework.[48]

MANAGING WITHOUT BEING A MICROMANAGER

In most homes, the wife acts as manager over the house and children.[49] Sometimes this works out, and sometimes it's an ongoing source of resentment between them. While some women enjoy the feeling of competence that comes from balancing children, housework, and sometimes outside work,[50] many would vote to give up this role.

> **ANN**: *I feel like I have two children, my three-year-old daughter and my husband. Both of them seem to need me to tell them what to do. I really wish my husband would just look around and see what needs to be done rather than always expect me to be the one to give him directions. It's really exhausting.*

Many men wait for instructions around housework and this puts their wives in a difficult bind. Because most men are sensitive to feeling subordinate, they resist or get defensive if their wives make demands of them, especially if the expectation is to get to the task immediately. On the other hand, many wives complain that if they don't act as household manager, they're forced to live with their husbands' far lower standards of cleanliness and parental involvement.[51]

Given these constraints, some mothers have found that if they want family work to be done to their standards, they need to be in the managerial role in a way that doesn't leave their husbands feeling shamed or inadequate.[52] Again, from a fairness standpoint, this arrangement isn't necessarily fair. More than one female client has complained to me, "It's bad enough I have to tell him what to do, I also have to be so nice about it when I'm doing it!" However, women who have both high expectations of their husbands' involvement, and who deliver those expectations with affection are the most successful in enacting change in their households.[53]

Women are sometimes hampered in their negotiations with men by being socialized to think that parenting is so inherently gratifying that they're not entitled to make any requests for compensation in time or help.[54] While many things in life are inherently rewarding, that doesn't mean that these acts shouldn't be counted as contributions if they benefit both members. In order to get your husband to do more, you have to become clear about the ways in which your own beliefs or behavior make you buy into your husband's communication or behavior.

Consider how you subtly or overtly diminish your bargaining power in your marriage:

> I'm not assertive enough.
> I feel too guilty to make demands.
> I feel intimidated by my husband's anger or threats.
> I believe that women should be responsible for the house and kids, no matter how little men do.

I give up too easily when we negotiate.

I don't know how to negotiate.

Lazy Husband Excuses

Many people don't have the skills needed to negotiate in marriage and many women get shut down before the negotiation even gets under way. It's useful to have a few responses for when this occurs. For example, Ruth and John have a transitional marriage. While they both agree that she should do more for the house and kids than he, she wants him to do a lot more than he's doing.

> COMMON LAZY HUSBAND EXCUSE #1
> *"I EARN MORE THAN YOU AND THEREFORE
> SHOULDN'T HAVE TO DO ANYTHING WHEN
> I GET HOME."*

Among other principles, Ruth should begin by appealing to his sense of fairness.

RUTH: It's true that I earn less than you but that doesn't mean my time is worth less. I also work hard and it isn't fair to me that I have to do everything.

JOHN: Yes, but if it weren't for me, we couldn't have the lifestyle that we have.

RUTH: I acknowledge that, John, and I also appreciate our lifestyle. However, I don't think that just because society doesn't value parenting and housework, that means that I never get a chance to rest.

COMMON LAZY HUSBAND EXCUSE #2
"I'M TOO TIRED TO HELP."

JOHN: You don't know how exhausted I am. I can't do one more thing when I get home. My job is much more stressful than yours.

In this scenario, Ruth should challenge that he's more exhausted than she, and challenge the principle that his work is more stressful.

RUTH: I do know how exhausted you are, though I don't think it's true that your job is any more stressful than mine. In some ways, your job is less stressful because you get to be around other adults while I'm with needy children far more than you. Either way, we both work during the day, and I'd like more help when you're home.

Ruth could also suggest that John take on tasks that aren't stressful like cleaning up the dinner dishes, giving the children baths, or putting the children to bed.[55]

COMMON LAZY HUSBAND EXCUSE #3
"I DON'T KNOW HOW."

JOHN: I'm just not good at all of this domestic stuff, you know that. It doesn't come naturally to me. Plus, you know how much I hate doing housework.

In this scenario Ruth should challenge the notion that he would have to be good at housework in order to do it.

RUTH: I understand that it doesn't come naturally to you, but you'll get the hang of it. I can show you how for the first few times. I wasn't that good doing some of the things I had to learn how to do, too. (In addition she should challenge the idea that he shouldn't have to do it if he hates it.) Well, I don't know many people who love housework, but it's gotta get done. So how can we make it more fair to both of us?

COMMON LAZY HUSBAND EXCUSE #4
"I CONTRIBUTE IN OTHER WAYS. I SHOULDN'T HAVE TO DO BOTH."

Again, Ruth should begin by appreciating.

RUTH: I do appreciate what you contribute. But I don't want to be the only one doing all of the parenting and housework. I never agreed to that.

Here again, if the goal is more involvement, Ruth shouldn't expect perfection from John. Instead, she should show appreciation for each step forward with the long-term goal of increased involvement. Behaviorists call this shaping behavior.[56] Shaping behavior is where you make rewards for every small change in a positive direction. Experimental psychologist B. F. Skinner came to fame in the 1960s for teaching pigeons to spin like tops by rewarding them every time they made a small move in the direction of a desired behavior.[57] I find this a useful technique when working with women to get their husbands to stop being

Lazy Husbands. In other words, constantly show appreciation for any small behavior that's new and improved.

Let's look at another couple. Becky and Sean have a deal that whoever cooks doesn't have to clean up the dinner dishes. While both work, Becky gets home an hour before Sean, so she ends up cooking most of the meals on the weekdays. Most of the time Sean gets the dishes done before he goes to bed, but sometimes he waits and does them before he goes to work in the morning. And occasionally he leaves them until he gets home from work that day. While Becky can almost tolerate them being left overnight, she has made it clear that she doesn't want them left around for the next day.

Recently, Sean left the dishes after dinner and Becky had Sean promise that he'd do the dishes before he went to work, reminding him that she doesn't like to come home to a sink full of dishes. However, Sean realized when he got up the next morning that he didn't have as much time as he needed, and decided to do the dishes when he came home that night. He didn't negotiate this with Becky, rather he hoped he could get out of the house before she got downstairs to observe it. However, as he left the bathroom to head downstairs, Becky said, "Don't forget you promised to do the dishes before you left." Sean knew he had promised that he'd do the dishes, but had hoped to get out of the house before it became clear that he hadn't. After Becky's reminder Sean could have:

➤ refused to do the dishes and left anyway
➤ apologized to Becky, acknowledged that he'd broken a promise, and offered to make it up to her if she let him skip out on his promise

➤ recognized that he'd promised her, done the dishes, and been late for work

Each scenario carries its own potential conflicts. If Sean had left after Becky's reminder, she would be fair to label this a hostile act, albeit a small one. It would be reasonable for her to have a serious talk with him that evening, and let him know that he undermines her feelings of closeness to him when he doesn't follow through on his promises. This conversation might go something like this:

BECKY: You know, Sean, I know it's only dishes and that it's not a big deal to you, but you know that I don't like to have dishes in the sink all day long.

SEAN: I hardly ever do it.

BECKY: Actually, it happens a lot. But you did promise me, and I'd like to feel you'll do the things you say you'll do.

SEAN: Give me a break. It's just this one time.

BECKY: It isn't, but that's not even the point. The point is that you told me you'd do them before we went to bed and you promised me before you left. I just want to feel you'll do the things you say you'll do. You got the benefit of having a meal prepared for you, and I'd like the benefit of not having to come home to a sink full of dishes.

The way in which this conversation goes from here will depend on Sean's maturity and Becky's ability to maintain a productive tone of voice despite Sean's provocations. I want Becky to lodge her complaint because I want Sean to know that he has to take her objections seriously. Hopefully, this interaction will

be embarrassing or awkward enough that he won't want to re-
peat it in the future. Again, Becky should be firm and *affectionate* in this interaction. Her goal isn't to shame Sean but rather
to let him know that *every time he skips out on his promises they
will have a conversation about it.* For many men, that prospect
alone motivates them to be more conscientious.

However, what if the interaction plays out with Sean wanting to make a deal with Becky about the dishes rather than
skipping out on doing them? This scenario might go like this:

SEAN: I'm really running late. Do you care if I just do the
dishes tonight?

Here Becky could either hold the line or barter. If Sean commonly breaks his deals with her, she should probably err on the
side of being a little tougher. That response would go like this.

BECKY: C'mon. You know our deal. Don't put me in the position
of having to be the policeman.
SEAN: I know, you're right. I thought I'd have enough time but
I'm running really late.
BECKY: Fine, but then tonight you get to do dinner and cleanup.

Becky has more leverage here because Sean's the one who's
backing out of a promise. Telling Sean that he has to do both
dinner and cleanup allows her to use her leverage to create something more equitable in exchange for the inconvenience of having the dishes remain unwashed. Obviously, Becky should show
more flexibility and restraint if Sean rarely breaks his promises
to her.

Sex

The comedian Chris Rock said, "Men only care about three things: food, sex, and silence!"[58] While there may be a few other things, sex is a subject that men think and talk about endlessly. Men, on average, rate sexual frequency as one of the top causes of marital satisfaction, whereas it's ranked much lower for the average woman.[59]

An example of this was shown when researchers paid attractive female and male college students to go up to college students of the opposite sex and ask them if they'd like to go home with them and fool around.[60] Practically none of the female coeds responded favorably to this offer, however, a hearty 75 percent of the males responded in the affirmative. Surprised? Me neither. Sex for men is a scarce resource. Frustrating to many men, a guy can't just go out and get sex whenever he wants it. It's a different story for women, as this study shows. They may not love the options of who they get to choose from, but they can generally have sex if that's the goal.

This difference in availability produces different feelings and attitudes about sex for men versus women. For example, from a reproductive standpoint, women's interests are best served by choosing the right partner, protecting themselves when they're pregnant, and then protecting those offspring once they arrive. Sex is less important as a means to pass on their genes once a pregnancy or a child arrives. This isn't to say that there aren't a lot of other reasons why sex still matters to women, or reasons why having sex is still in their reproductive best interests in these situations.[61] However, from an evolutionary standpoint, men who were preoccupied with sex were more likely to see opportunities to pass on their genes than those who were less interested.

I highlight these differences because I often hear my women friends or clients voice some measure of disgust or exasperation with their husband's desire for or preoccupation with sex.

> RHONDA: *Lonnie is just on me all the time. It sort of disgusts me. I just feel like, "I'm not a dog, you know. You can't just hump me whenever you're in the mood!"*

> LONNIE: *Rhonda acts like if I want to make love to her I'm just using her. My attitude is like, "Um, excuse me. I am married to you, you know. Remember? Father of your children? I'm not some frat boy who's just trying to get you in the backseat of his Chevy."*

Finally, as we've seen, men don't always express or receive love in the same way as do women. Men are more likely to do both through activities (earning money, washing the car, moving stuff around).[62] An important one of these activities is having sex. Men commonly experience and express their deepest and most tender emotions through making love.

> PHIL: *Colleen doesn't get this but I feel the most in touch with my love for her while we're making love. It's also when I know more than ever that she loves me. If we go for a month or so without making love I just start feeling really disconnected from her.*

Women are more likely to want to talk about their emotions, and want to hear a man talk about his before she'll be in the mood.[63] In fact, many women say that talking is a turn-on whereas few men would say this, and many would say the opposite.

> URSULA: *I don't like to just jump into it. I need a little romance, a little appreciation, a little talking about feelings. My husband doesn't need any of that to be raring to go.*

Of course there are many, many reasons why women lose interest in sex after they become mothers. In addition to exhaustion, nursing mothers experience a decrease in mood because the hormone prolactin shuts downs their sexual desire. And your husband's laziness probably isn't the biggest turn-on in the world either. While most men can still make love when they are mad at their wives, few women feel sexual when they're mad at their husbands. This is because avoiding sex with someone you're mad at makes good evolutionary sense for a woman. Nature may have paired "being mad at partner" with "lack of interest in sex" because those women who didn't connect the two may have ended up raising their children alone. Therefore, stress and anger are more likely to shut a woman down while they don't for the male, who is wired by evolution to be ready whenever opportunity strikes.

So why all of this talk about sex and men? Because many women make the mistake of withdrawing from sex once they become mothers. They become permanently preoccupied with their kids and insufficiently preoccupied with their husband's happiness. If you're the one with the low sexual desire, I won't promise that having sex will, by itself, motivate your husband to scrub the toilets all of a sudden and volunteer to make the school lunches. A more likely outcome is that a semiactive sex life will contribute to the right environment for creating change. As I have said repeatedly, women who create the most change, among other qualities, act in a way that is both authoritative and *affectionate*. For men, an important aspect of their needs to express and receive affection are done through sex.

Of course, this works the other way, too, and perhaps more profoundly. Marital researcher John Gottman found that when men do more housework, their wives feel more interested in them sexually.[64] For women, a husband who does housework not only provides her with relief from stress and exhaustion, he also shows her that he cares about her and what's important to her. It's probably also true that when women make love to their husbands, men feel a lot more in the mood to demonstrate their feelings of affection with housework than they did before.

STRATEGIES AROUND SEX

Psychiatrist Frank Pittman advises couples to have sex at least once a week "whether they feel like it or not."[65] This is similar advice to that given by marriage therapist Michele Weiner-Davis, who recommends among other strategies, "the Nike approach to sex; in other words, 'Just Do It.' "[66] Since women may need more ideal conditions to be in the mood, deciding to have sex regardless of your mood may be key to increasing or maintaining marital harmony and cooperation with your husband. Many women find that while they may not be in the mood in the beginning, they can become interested in sex once they get going. As Weiner-Davis states, "Knowing why you're not so interested in sex won't boost your desire. Doing something about it will."[67]

In addition to the Nike solution, Weiner-Davis recommends acting on fleeting thoughts about sex, paying attention to what turns you on and when, behaving in a more sexual way through dress and attitude, and taking care of your partner's needs if you're not in the mood.

> **GWEN:** *I like sex, but I'm definitely a lot less interested since I became a mom. Will and I used to fight a lot about it until I decided that everything goes better if I make a commitment to make love with him once or twice a week. Typically, I'm not in the mood when we start but I get into it after a while. And he's such an easier person to live with, it's worth pushing myself in this area a little bit.*

MAKE SURE YOU'RE GETTING ENOUGH REST AND SUPPORT

This is a tall order for most mothers these days, especially working moms. It's also a good reason to consider relaxing some of your standards with housework, and getting your husband to do more around the house. It's possible that if your husband sees the connection between your exhaustion and your lack of sexual desire he may become more motivated to do some of the things you've been wanting him to do.

WORRY ABOUT THE KIDS

Many moms can't relax enough to be interested in sex because they're too worried about the children coming in the room or overhearing the lovemaking. With younger children, sex can be timed around naps or once they're down for the evening. As children get older they can be instructed that mom and dad want "private time." If your kids sleep in the same bed as you, wait till they fall asleep and consider using other parts of the house.

DEPRESSION

Postpartum depression occurs in some 10 to 15 percent of women and can last for several years after an infant's birth.[68] However, depression from any cause is a sex killer. If you have been depressed, you should get an evaluation and help from a qualified doctor or psychiatrist. Common treatments include medication and counseling, with the combination of the two showing the greatest effect.

WORK ON THE ROMANCE

Since women often need romance to get going sexually, make sure you and your husband have opportunities to be close and intimate. I would say, without exception, that every couple who shows up in my practice for marriage therapy fails to schedule weekly time for romance. No wonder they feel as if there's no love between them! Bearing this in mind, schedule a weekly or biweekly date for just the two of you. Agree not to talk about problems for the whole night of your date. Agree to do something that you both find pleasurable. If you disagree on what's fun, take turns choosing on alternate weekends.

CONSIDER YOUR PAST

As we saw in previous chapters, our past commonly affects our present-day behavior in marriage. If you were molested, abused, or treated in any other way that affected your fundamental feelings of safety in the world, this may be affecting your sexuality. Make sure you're getting adequate help and support to deal with those issues.

BUT WHAT IF HE'S THE ONE WITH THE LOW SEX DRIVE?

If he's the one with low desire, you should work to be empathic toward him as a first step toward change. While men are less likely to withdraw from sex out of anger, some do. Men are far less likely to bring conflicts to the table than are women. Therefore, try to engage him in a conversation about his feelings and see if your sexual relationship is something he's willing to work on.

> **EVE:** *I always hear about men complaining that their wives never want to make love to them. I've got the opposite problem, Howie never wants to make love to me. He says that it doesn't have anything to do with his feelings for me and maybe it doesn't, but it still really bothers me.*

Some men also have a hard time seeing their wives in a sexual way once they become mothers. If this is the case, encourage him to talk about this. If he can't make the transition, consider talking to a couples therapist about it. If none of these are successful in increasing your partner's desire, work toward accepting your differences and prioritizing what's good in your life and marriage.

◆

Understanding the subtle and not-so-subtle differences between men's and women's behavior can be an important tool in creating change. Differences in communication, expressing feelings, the role of status, and differences in sexual desire are present in almost every marriage and relationship. Learning what can be changed and how it can be changed is essential to marital happiness and to motivating your partner to care more about what is important to you.

Okay, there's one more tool in this arsenal, and that is the next chapter, written for your husband. If he's like many men, he may find the idea of reading a self-help book about as appealing as a long-drawn-out discussion about feelings. Bearing that in mind, ask him to read the next chapter as a favor to you. If he resists that, ask him to read the first page. Once he sees that the book isn't anti-guy, he'll probably finish it, and see that some of the ways that you want him to change don't take that much work or rewiring. He may even be inspired to read the whole book. Okay, maybe that's asking too much. But it's reasonable to ask him to read one page and see if it piques his interest.

For the Husband

The Lazy Husband? *How about a book
called* The Bitchy Wife?

—QUESTION POSED TO AUTHOR BY MALE

Okay, right now I'm sure I'm the last person you want to take advice from. Your wife has not so subtly left *The Lazy Husband* out on the night-stand (your side) and has quoted me so many times you've more than once seriously considered looking up where I live and paying me a little visit. I understand, honest I do. That's why I didn't include my address.

I know that laziness is a matter of perspective. When I don't jump up to help my wife clear the table because I'm more en-grossed in reading the paper and less grossed out by the dishes in the sink, it's not laziness on my part, it's relaxation. And I really, *really* like to relax. But there is a cost, and overall, if seven-teen years of marriage has taught me anything, it's that it's not worth the bill. But maybe that's just me. On the other hand, if your wife is reading a book called *The Lazy Husband,* maybe a few suggestions from a Lazy Husband in recovery could improve your situation at home, or at least, get her off your back.

Just so you know that we're on the same page, even though the book is titled *The Lazy Husband,* I haven't ruled out the possibility that your wife may be really difficult. In addition, I don't necessarily think that it's all about *you* changing. I spent the prior seven chapters telling her how to take responsibility for how she contributes to the problems by either taking over, being critical, expecting too much, not understanding her past, not appreciating the ways you *do* contribute to her and the family, and misunderstanding how gender differences create problems. I told her that *the best way to change your partner is to change yourself.*

But the same goes for us. So in this chapter I'm going to suggest a lot of not-so-difficult things that you can begin doing right away to improve your situation. Small, sometimes unbelievably small, adjustments in workload or appreciation can make a world of difference to your wife and to your marriage.

Housework and Sex

Sex is a subject that is near and dear to most men's hearts. It's often one of the most important predictors for men's satisfaction in marriage. So why do some men have wives who want to get it on while others don't? Marital researcher John Gottman made an interesting discovery: women are more interested in having sex when they're married to men who are more willing to do housework.[1] Why would putting your hands into dishwater make your wife more interested in putting her hands on you?

A good sex life makes men feel important, cared about, and

connected to their wives. For women, a good sex life is further down the list below a man's affection, caring, communication, and his interest in the kids and house.[2] While sex is in the female gumbo of marital satisfaction, it ain't the main ingredient. As Gottman writes in *Why Marriages Succeed or Fail,* "Housework may seem like a trivial concern compared to sexuality, but women see it as a major issue affecting their sex life. Treating your wife as a servant will almost inevitably affect the more intimate, fragile parts of a relationship. Being the sole person to clean the toilet is definitely not an aphrodisiac!"[3]

Why the difference between the genders? Because sex isn't scarce for women. Almost any woman could walk out the door and find a guy to have sex with her within a matter of hours. She may not love the choices, but she wouldn't have much problem making it happen. What's scarce for women isn't a man who's willing to have sex—it's a man who's willing to help raise children, do housework, talk about his feelings, and be affectionate. Therefore, when a guy does housework it has several effects on a woman's sexuality. The first is that it makes her feel cared about. It's a way of saying, "No, you're not in this marriage to serve me and clean up after me. I'm not going to dump everything on you. I care enough about you to do my share."

This is also important to a woman's desire because *it decreases her stress levels.* Women's sexual interest is tied to stress for evolutionary reasons. Since women only ovulate once a month, they have a very finite number of opportunities to spread their genes over the course of their lifetimes. They are right to be more conservative about choosing a man who will increase the likelihood of those offspring surviving.

Men, theoretically, can spread their genes on a daily basis.

Therefore, from an evolutionary perspective, men worry less about their offspring surviving, and more about maximizing the opportunities to spread their genes. So men's sexual interest isn't bothered by such trivial distractions as mood, energy level, stress, or whether or not we even like the person—whereas for women, these concerns are typically more central. The moral of this story is that if you feel dissatisfied with how little your wife wants to have sex with you, the first action isn't to purchase something from the Victoria's Secret catalogue, it's to look at your feelings about the toilet bowl.

BUT I CAN'T MEET HER STANDARDS FOR HOUSEWORK

I understand. She sees dirt where you see nothing, she sees chaos where you see order, she feels tormented by dishes in the sink while you just see dishes in the sink. And then, when you do go to do it, you get told that you don't do it right. Maybe she is too controlling or her standards aren't very reasonable. That's a possibility that I went over in the prior chapters where I suggested that she may have to consider reducing her standards with parenting and housework, among other behaviors, if she wants more out of you—a fact which there are many studies to support.

But since I've got your attention, let's consider the possibility that you use her high standards against her as a way to get out of housework. Not that I myself personally would ever *dream* of doing such a manipulative, devious act to my beloved wife. I have *never* said that I can't do laundry, get the kids dressed, or clean the bathroom because she complains that I mix the whites with the colors, don't match the kid's clothing correctly, or miss huge spots in the bathroom. And I have *never,* nor would I *ever* consider the fact that if I do a half-assed job that maybe, just maybe, she might, in exasperation, take it over herself, thereby freeing up time for me to do all of the other things I do enjoy doing, none of which have the vaguest relationship to housework (or sometimes, parenting).

The reality is that if I can get my wife to do most things that I don't want to do, I will let her do them faster than you can say *dust bunny.* But even *I* have my limits on how much I'll refuse to do, and I've changed those limits much further in the direction of doing more over the years as I've seen the marriage get better each time that I do.

So if you're with me so far, consider this suggestion. Sit down with her within the next few days and tell her that *you are willing to begin doing things differently around the house.* This doesn't mean that you're going to sign on to everything she suggests, nor does it mean that she's going to accept any small change from you as the second coming. You're saying, "I understand that this is really important to you, and your happiness is important to me. Because of those two facts, I'm glad to think about ways that I can do more around the house." Use those exact words. "I understand that this is really important to you, and your happiness is important to me. Because of those two facts, I'm glad to think about ways that I can do more around the house."

➤ **WRITE OUT A LIST WITH HER OF WHAT SHE'D LIKE YOU TO DO**. If you think she underestimates what you do already, write out a list of what you're currently doing with the house or for the family. Do not make this a tit-for-tat fight! At this point, the goal is to cooperatively and affectionately begin to brainstorm ideas for going forward in a more productive way. It is absolutely not to have a fight about who's doing what for whom.

➤ **SEE IF THERE ARE BARGAINS THAT CAN BE MADE.** It may be hugely important for her if you do laundry once a week and that may make her a lot more willing to have you play basketball on Saturday mornings without complaining. My point is that there's almost always a win-win solution in every household, and in most situations. Bearing this in mind, think of what you'd like to see in your house or marriage and begin trading off some housework, or being a more involved parent in order to get it. Bear in mind that you're not going to get a hundred dollars for offering to trade ten. If you want to barter for something you really want, it has to be fair market value for what she wants.

➤ **DON'T FIGHT WITH HER SO MUCH.** Another one of Gottman's discoveries were that couples who had the best marriages were those where the husband didn't fight his wife's influence.[4] Those homes where the husband stubbornly insisted on being right all of the time, or insisted on always getting his way, were rated as far less satisfying by *both* members of the couple. Bearing this in mind, experiment with giving in more. Don't see it as a power struggle or a principled matter of right and wrong. As the saying goes, "In marriage, you can be right or you can be happy, but sometimes you can't be both!"

On the other hand, maybe you need to learn how to be stronger with your wife and not let her run over you so much. In this case, your refusing to do housework or parenting may be an attempt to lodge a protest against how you feel mistreated by her. Men are far more likely to retreat from parenting, for example, when they are in unhappy marriages.[5] If this is the case, it's probably better to work toward being more direct with your complaints about her than withdrawing from being a dad. While it *is* a way to get back at her, it also hurts your relationship with your kids, something that has long-term consequences for them *and* you.

This dynamic existed for Don and Sandy. Don entered marriage without knowing how to be assertive in marriage. He grew up in a house where he was ignored by his parents and brought a feeling of unimportance into his marriage. His wife had the opposite problem. She grew up in a household with five sisters who were harsh and competitive. She learned early on that if you want to get something in a relationship, you better push hard or you'll get walked on. She was drawn to Don because she interpreted his passivity as a willingness to give to her and not compete with her.

While Don was drawn to Sandy's assertiveness, he didn't know how to manage her as they began to enter the rocky years of child rearing where each felt deprived of time and energy. Sandy's attitude was that if you want something in life, you push hard for it, and it all comes out in the wash. Don's attitude was that if you wait and hope, the other may eventually care enough about you to give to you. Unfortunately, Sandy's unregulated assertiveness and Don's unregulated passivity locked them into a bad marital dynamic where he resented her dominance and control, and she resented his passive-agressive behavior. The only way that Don knew how to fight against Sandy was to withdraw from her in the arenas that he knew were important to her, which, not surprisingly, infuriated Sandy.

When Don entered therapy, he needed help learning how to reverse this dynamic. To do this, Don needed to learn how to:

➤ be more direct with his requests
➤ be more direct with his complaints
➤ work on his unconscious beliefs that interfered with his getting what he wanted in marriage
➤ become less fearful of Sandy's anger, disappointment, or judgment

If this sounds like you, you may be helped by making some of the same changes as Don.

Examine Your Childhood

Whether you tend to be too aggressive or too passive, you should work to understand how your childhood caused you to take the position that you've taken in marriage. If you feel like you're in a power struggle with your wife, assume that you're half of the problem. Make a commitment to change what you're doing, regardless of what she does or doesn't do. Make this an act of your own integrity. Consider the possibility that her complaints about you may have a grain of truth to them, even if they're not the whole loaf.[6] If she calls you a lazy slob, maybe that's hugely unfair and inappropriate. On the other hand, maybe you are a bit more of a slacker than you admit to being. Again, if she's having you read this chapter, assume that there's something in the marriage that she wants you to change that really may be worth changing. You can always go back to your old ways if you want. But you may find out that there's gold hidden under all of those rocks, weeds, and dirt.

Parenting

There's a big trend for fathers to be more involved than dads of prior generations.[7] As with housework, it's possible that if you're not superinvolved in your children's lives, it's partly because your wife is overinvolved. In earlier chapters, I described the research that shows men tend to withdraw from parenting when women are overly directive or controlling. However, there are common differences between how men and women parent, regardless of the mother's behavior.

To review the highlights, men tend to respond less quickly to children's frustrations or cries of distress. They are also more likely to want their children to have experiences that emphasize risk and adventure than are women. Men are also less likely to experience as many changes in identity with the birth of a child. As a result of these differences, many marriages get into trouble when these differences aren't respected. A common scenario is that a woman feels troubled by her husband's lower level of responsiveness, and reacts with criticism or excessive direction. The husband, who already feels somewhat less informed or experienced as a parent, defers to his wife, but also feels criticized and shamed by her complaints. As a result, he withdraws from being a parent.

If this has been the case for you, it's very important that you and your wife put the parenting onto a different track. Children who are raised by involved fathers do better in life, have a greater sense of emotional security, and are far closer to their fathers when they're older than children raised by uninvolved fathers.[8] I commonly see older men in my practice who were uninvolved with their children, and want a closer relationship with them now that they're grown. Unfortunately, the adult children not infrequently say something like, "Thanks, but no thanks. Where were you when I needed you?"

Bearing this in mind, *tell your wife that you'd like to be more involved as a parent, but that you would like less involvement from her.* This should be done in an affectionate rather than a confrontational manner. Explain that when she supervises, complains, or criticizes your parenting, it makes you feel like giving up and turning it over to her.

Tell her that you'd like the opportunity to make your own mistakes in parenting and (with a smile on your face) she can offer her feedback *if you request it.* For example, many mothers freak out when their husbands watch the football game while the toddler is crawling around at his feet. They feel the child is being neglected unless actively being engaged in direct play with the parent. Those women are wrong about that. Unless the child is in some danger, he or she can still have a good day with dad even if dad isn't actively involved in the same kind of face-to-face that mom would give.

Daily Appreciations

One of the absolute best and easiest things you can do for your marriage is to appreciate everything that your wife does for you, the kids, or the house. I mean *every freaking thing.* Here's a common list if nothing comes to mind:

KIDS

making doctor's appointments
arranging play dates
buying their clothes
talking with them about their feelings
giving them baths or attending to their cleanliness
helping with homework
guiding their religious or spiritual development
taking them to whatever after-school activities they have
thinking about their psychological well-being

HOUSE

laundry
cooking
cleaning
food shopping
dishes
making repairs
organizing
gardening

TAKING CARE OF YOU

arranging doctor's appointments
buying clothes
talking with you about your life
improving your social life

Appreciation is important for many reasons. First of all, it's a way of saying that you don't take her for granted. Even if the two of you have an arrangement where you always do x and she always does y, you should still show appreciation each time she does y. I often hear men say, "I shouldn't have to appreciate it when she makes me dinner or puts the kids to bed. That's our *arrangement*." Wrong, wrong, and furthermore, wrong. Appreciations are a way of telling her that you love her. In fact, many studies show that even if a husband isn't doing his fair share, simply beginning to appreciate his wife for all of the things that she does greatly increases her satisfaction with her marriage.[9] And if your wife is satisfied with the marriage, odds are much greater that you're going to be satisfied with the marriage. And if she's dissatisfied with the marriage, well, we all know what that's like.

Some men don't give appreciations because they feel it has to be a big production. However, appreciations can be short and to the point. Here are a few examples:

Thanks for making dinner, that was great. I appreciate it.

Thanks for getting the kids to bed, honey. I appreciate it.

Thanks for making my doctor's appointment. That was sweet of you.

Thanks for keeping the house so clean. I really like it.

Thanks for not getting mad when I was late. That meant a lot to me.

Thanks for apologizing after the fight. That was generous of you.

Thanks for being such a great mother. It brings me a lot of joy to watch you with them.

APPRECIATING HER FOR HERSELF

You should also strive to appreciate aspects of her that she likes about herself. For example:

What traits of your wife are the most meaningful to her?
   her career
   her capacity as a mother
   her capacity as a wife
   her ability to be a good:
      friend
      daughter
   her intelligence
   her sense of humor
   her organizing ability
   her athleticism

We feel the most loved by our partners when they appreciate what we value about ourselves. However, we also feel loved when they strive to avoid hurting us in the areas where we're the most sensitive. For example, Marina felt very insecure about her weight. Even though she was average for her height, she often experienced herself as weighing ten to fifteen pounds more than her ideal. Her husband, Paul, knew that this was a sore spot for Marina, and so he'd say, "No, you're perfect. You don't need to lose any weight," whenever she asked him about it. Paul's saying this made Marina feel loved because it helped her to not be hard on herself, something which she struggled to achieve. If Paul had said, "Then lose some weight and quit bitching about it!" Marina would have felt rejected by Paul, resentful of his criticism, and left alone to fend with her own harsh feelings about herself.

In other words, there are opportunities every day to either increase the happiness and closeness between you and your wife or decrease it. If you're like most men, you have a lot more power than you give yourself credit for. Bearing this in mind, consider the following exercise.

Think about your wife's areas of vulnerability. What are the areas where she is the most likely to feel guilt, anxiety, or self-criticism?

weight

parenting

desire to be a good wife (this is probably important to her even if you don't think it is)

relationship to her mother or father

job

IQ

struggles with friends

her relationship with your parents or relatives

Bearing these in mind, how often do you make reassuring comments about the areas where she has the most anxiety or self-criticism?

frequently

occasionally

not at all

Make a commitment to spontaneously compliment and/or reassure her several times a week in these areas.

But what if I can't stand something about her?

It's true that it's harder to be supportive about behaviors that you're unhappy about.

> **VICTOR**: *Harriet always wants me to reassure her that she's a great mother but it's hard for me to do because I don't think she's such a great mother. She's critical of the kids and blows up at them for really stupid things. Then if I don't reassure her that she's a great mother, she blows up at me!*

WHAT SHOULD VICTOR DO?

Victor should still find ways to support Harriet's mothering, even if he feels really critical of her. If Harriet is already critical of herself, his criticizing her will only make her behavior with the kids worse rather than better. Overall, the more self-critical we are, the more likely we are to react in ways that are problematic. In the last chapter, I advised your wife to 'catch you doing something right' and praise that rather than focusing on the negative. Same applies for you.

If you feel critical of your wife's behavior, don't voice it as a criticism. Instead, compliment her whenever she does it right. In this case, I instructed Victor to say things to Harriet like, "Wow, I was really impressed with how cool you were when the girls were going crazy today. That was great." Or "You were really sweet with the girls this evening, they were eating it up!" This doesn't mean that you can never complain about your wife. Just know that if you're wading into an area where she already has a lot of self-hatred or doubt, you should use kid gloves and err on the positive.

YEAH, BUT WHAT IF SHE'S DOING SOMETHING THAT REALLY BUGS ME?

Good question. Marriage isn't just about emphasizing the positive, it's also about finding ways to air complaints in a productive manner. Studies show that conversations almost always end the way they begin.[10] Thus, if you start out a conversation with, "You know what I hate about you?" there is an excellent probability that you'll end the conversation hearing what your wife hates about you, too. Which is fine if you go in for that sort of thing. Better to structure the complaint in the following way:

- ➤ begin with an appreciation
- ➤ say how serious it is on a scale of one to ten
- ➤ use nonblaming language
- ➤ take responsibility for your end of the problem
- ➤ ask for solutions
- ➤ thank her for listening

Let's look at an example. Larry hated Paula's spending habits. While they both earned a decent income, he couldn't stand the fact that she refused to live within a budget, and acted as though they had much more money than they had. Bearing in mind the points above, Larry structured the conversation as follows:

APPRECIATION: Paula, I really appreciate your love for life and I know that your spending is a part of that. You feel like life is short and we should go for it and not be so worried about money. There's a lot about that that I admire.

EFFECT: Lets Paula know that he understands her motivation and even respects aspects of it.

LEVEL OF SERIOUSNESS: But I want to have a conversation about our spending habits. On a scale of one to ten, this is probably an eight for me, so I think it's really important that we come to some kind of resolution around it.

EFFECT: Tells Paula to pay close attention and take him seriously.

USE NONBLAMING LANGUAGE: I feel worried that we don't have a budget and that you haven't wanted to live with one. It makes me feel worried that we're never going to have a retirement and that we're living way beyond our means.

EFFECT: Lets Paula know what his concerns are without making her feel bad about herself.

TAKE RESPONSIBILITY FOR YOUR PART: I know that I probably worry too much about money, but I still think this is important.

EFFECT: Lets her know that his goal isn't to humiliate her, and that he's not perfect. Has the effect of equalizing the interaction rather than putting him above her.

ASK FOR SOLUTIONS: So what do you think we can do to work together on this one?

EFFECT: Reminds Paula that they're in this together, it's solvable, and that he expects a different path.

THANK HER FOR LISTENING: I appreciate you talking with me about this. I know you don't like this topic very much, and that we have really different ideas around it.

EFFECT: Keeps it positive. Reinforces her willingness to be sensitive to him and to his needs in the future. Increases trust in the marriage rather than reduces it.

DON'T BE SO DEFENSIVE

Nobody likes to be criticized and it's human nature to get your back up when you are. I think marriages go best when men don't get so upset about their wives' criticisms. It's strong to remain calm and in control. When my kids were young I learned a lot by observing my friend Dale. I would sometimes watch his wife list a bunch of things she wanted him to do, or complain about things he hadn't done, while he patiently and quietly listened with a loving smile on his face. When she was done, he'd say, "Okay, honey. I can do that." His wife would smile and say thanks and they were done with it. I was amazed. At that time, my response to similar behaviors from my wife was to get self-righteous and hostile about what I already was doing and why she had no right to ask me to do any more. I had never imagined that simply listening, being affectionate, and not getting defensive could be such a position of strength, and be so effective. But I learned. It took me about ten years, but I learned.

So ask questions. Assume there's something worth hearing in the criticism even if you're not wild about the way it's presented. The more you hear her out, the sooner the storm will pass and the happier she'll be with you.

THE DOWNLOAD

I have observed that it's common for women to want to download their day when reconnecting with their husbands when they both get home. Often, this means talking about the worries, stresses, and complaints they have about the house, children, friends, work, whatever—topics that problem-solving men have a hard time hearing about in much detail. Because this appears to be such a common area of stress, I recommend that you make a regular practice of greeting your wife with a hug, and just listening to her without comment for at least ten to fifteen minutes every day. You may be bored by what she has to say. In the words of Stuart Smalley, "And that's okay."[11] I guarantee you that she's not really hanging on to every one of your words, even when she acts like she is.

The secret to marital success isn't voicing every rude thought or reaction you have. It comes from being interested in the same way you would a coworker or friend who tells you something that's really important to them, and not all that interesting to you. I stress this not just for her well-being but for yours. If your wife believes that her feelings matter to you, she'll be much happier and easier to live with. If she feels as if she has to fight to get your attention, then she's going to fight with you to get your attention, and resent all of the imperfect parts of you—aspects that will recede far into the background if she feels cared about.

THE STONE WALL

Men are more likely to shut down and withdraw when they feel criticized by their wives. This is an effort to contain strong feelings of shame, anger, or rejection. Stonewalling is a serious problem in marriage because it is just the behavior that makes most women go nuts.[12] As I said in an earlier chapter, the marital dynamic that's most likely to lead to divorce is the distancer-pursuer dynamic. If you respond to conflict with your wife by shutting down, withdrawing, and refusing to talk about what's bothering you, you may be putting your marriage on a dangerous course. In fact, one study found that women prefer men who complain about them to men who withdraw; this is probably because men who complain look engaged in the marriage, while men who withdraw look as though they don't even care. So it's better not to withdraw so much, and use the principles I described in the step above about voicing your complaints. Most marriages don't end because of huge fights but because of a gradual and steady withdrawal.[13]

TALK ABOUT FEELINGS

Okay, for whatever reason, women really like it when we talk about our feelings. It's a way for them to connect to us and know us. Men have a harder time with this, especially around feelings that make them look or feel inadequate. This is unfortunate because many men miss out on an important source of support and love —their very own spouses. Bearing this in mind, experiment with disclosing more of your feelings to your wife. These might be anxieties you have about your work, your position in life, your friendships, your appearance, your abilities as a father or husband. While you may believe that it makes you look weak in your wife's eyes, it's likely that she'll view your willingness to talk about these aspects of yourself as a strength. Of course, you don't just have to talk about vulnerabilities. You can also talk about your kids, your career, your passion, whatever. Just talk more.

BE AFFECTIONATE

Women rank affection as one of the most important behaviors that they seek in a man.[14] Unfortunately, many men have a hard time with it. They were raised by fathers who weren't affectionate or by mothers who were either unaffectionate or too affectionate. Regardless, showing affection can make your marriage a much better place for both of you. Bearing this in mind,

> grab her hand while the two of you are walking down the street
> give her a daily hug
> offer her a massage at least once a week
> take her face in your hands and tell her how much you appreciate everything she does for you, the house, and the kids

Quit thinking about it and do it.

◆

Happiness in marriage comes when we take responsibility for how we contribute to the problems and then commit to work on ourselves. In general, men have happier marriages when we're active parents, participate in housework, show appreciation, don't withdraw, and are affectionate with our wives. The fact that your wife is reading my book is evidence that there are some adjustments the two of you may need to make to keep your marriage on track. Doing some of the suggestions in this chapter may be just enough to change her from thinking of you as a Lazy Husband to a Great Husband.

The Lazy Husband Campaign

The long-distance runner James Fixx once observed that people who end their runs before thirty minutes miss the best part of exercise. He noted that a run only really starts to get good *after* that because the body has had a chance to warm up and prepare itself for the stress and pleasure of it. I think the same can be said of marriage with children. Most divorces occur when children are young. This is tragic because those are the heavy lifting years, when couples have to figure out how to preserve a sense of self while giving everything, how to be sensitive to their partner's needs despite the changes that have occurred in him or her, and how to strike a balance between asking for what you want and not giving away the store.

There's a lot to figure out about what is and isn't fair in the division of labor with the house, kids, and finances, and this often takes years rather than months to understand. However I conclude with where I began: it's on men to do more of the changing. Despite the fact that there are many things that women could or should do differently in their relationships with men, the reality is that women are doing a lot more in most households and, overall, getting paid less.

Not only is it fair that men do more, it's also better for their children. Children who are raised by involved fathers make for a better society because they will most likely produce sons who want to be involved as dads. In addition, women raised by involved fathers will have higher expectations that their husbands will participate as fathers than women raised by dads who stood on the parental sidelines.

However, it's likely that women are going to continue be the prime movers and shakers in getting men to change. As sociologist Scott Coltrane writes, "If more wives want help from husbands to make things more fair, if more men feel pressure from their wives to do more, and if more mothers want fathers to be involved for the children's benefit, we will see more actual sharing of family work. All three attitudes have become more prevalent in the past decade, and are likely to increase even further."[1]

Let's look at some other trends to see where it's all headed. The current trend over the past few decades is for women to delay the birth of their first child.[2] This is important because women who delay becoming mothers are more likely to have careers and to therefore be in a better position to bargain and negotiate at home. In addition, women who are fully employed may be more motivated to be less controlling around child care and housework.

It's also likely that prioritizing the needs of our children is going to stay at present levels, if not increase in the future. This is because children are going to continue to require a lot of time, attention, and investment as the world that greets them continues to require more from them than prior generations.[3] In addition, the fact that parents are having fewer children means that parents are investing more in the few children that they have.

The belief that men should be involved as fathers is more prevalent in the popular culture, and may continue to be so.

Advertisements that glamorize fathering are more common today than in prior generations. For example, a ubiquitous Calvin Klein ad for cologne features a man laying on a beach with an infant against his chest. Other ads feature the man with his wife and child playing in the sand together. When the mother is featured in the commercial, the emphasis is less a portrait of madonna and child than padre and child. These ads speak of fatherhood as meaningful and desirable, not something that is solely in the province of women. However, there's still a long way to go as many ads still portray men as bumbling and in desperate need of wifely direction.[4]

I also see evidence of this shift toward valuing fatherhood in my conversations with fathers in my practice and in the neighborhood. When I was growing up, dads spent much of their weekends doing leisure activities that often had little to do with kids or family. However, many of today's dads have shifted their competitive energies off the golf course with their buddies into a host of weekend activities with their kids. Fathers who don't attend school functions, sporting events, or otherwise show an extra investment in their children's well-being may feel inadequate in discussions with fathers who are more involved. Thus, men may feel pressure not only from women to do more, but from men, too.

While today's father spends about six hours interacting with his school-aged children per weekend (much more than prior generations) it's mostly time spent in play and leisure, as it's been for decades.[5] The grunt work of changing diapers, preparing meals, taking the kids to the doctor, and giving baths is still being performed primarily by mothers. In other words, the activities that modern-day dads engage in are still strongly shaped by earlier expectations about what men and women *should* do, rather being shaped by a fair division of labor.[6]

But returning to the jogger's analogy, it's important to highlight that marriage is more like a marathon than a sprint. Changes that occur in marriage take place over many, many years. And the more that present-day behaviors and attitudes are influenced by our parents, our comparisons with others, and our outdated expectations, the slower those changes may be to occur. Despite his behavior, your husband probably really *does* want to make you happy. However, it's also likely that he is confused about what's fair to do with the house and kids based on social pressures about what it means to be a man, what he observed growing up, and what he observes from his peers. It's also likely that you have some confusion about this, and your confusion contributes to his.

People rarely change quickly. Bearing this in mind, plan on a lazy husband campaign with a long-term perspective. I emphasize this because some changes will occur slowly. Therefore, assume that you are going to make the following principles part of your core identity:

- ➤ a healthy sense of entitlement
- ➤ an expectation of change and cooperation (even when it's not immediately forthcoming)
- ➤ a commitment to appreciate whatever it is that he's doing right in the marriage
- ➤ a feeling of acceptance and compassion for who he is, regardless of whether he changes quickly or not

If you live by these simple principles your anger will decrease, your marriage will be better, and your husband will feel inspired to do more. Don't worry about the baby steps. As long as he's moving in the right direction, you are on your way to the kind of sharing you've always wanted and deserved!

Notes

INTRODUCTION

1. Hochschild (1989, p. 202) observed that women work an extra month a year more than men when family work is factored into the equation. As she writes in the *Second Shift*, women ". . . bear the weight of a contradiction between traditional ideology and modern circumstances. Unless they assume the extra work of changing the division of labor, it is usually they who work the extra month a year . . . If women lived in a culture that presumed active fatherhood, they wouldn't need to devise personal strategies to bring it about." University of Virginia family researcher E. Mavis Hetherington (2002) writes, "Apparently a generation of feminist rhetoric and wifely exhortation about the second shift has failed to penetrate the male world view: which is that men work and women keep house—everything else women do, including work, represents an 'in addition to.' Over two thirds of married women in our study complained about sharing a disproportionate burden of childcare and housework." Amato and Booth (1997) write on this topic, "It is likely that families in which fathers are highly involved are also those in which mothers are especially competent, caring, and encouraging of their husband's participation . . ." And Mahony (1995, p. 6) observes, "The good news is that the dream of real, practical equality between women and men isn't a dream anymore. Women can make it happen. The bad news is that it's up to women themselves. It isn't coming on any silver platter. Then again, maybe that's good news, too."
2. Pina and Bengston (1993).
3. Bird (1999); Kiecolt-Glaser and Newton (2001).
4. Radin and Graeme (1982).
5. C. P. Cowan and P. A. Cowan, cited in Hochschild (1989, p. 248).
6. Lovekin (2003) summarizes findings by sociologists Scott Coltrane, Ph.D., and Michele Adams, Ph.D.
7. Huber and Spitze (1983), cited in Hochschild (1989, p. 224).
8. Gottman (1994, p. 155).
9. Lovekin (2003). Also, Amato (1994, p. 1039) found that the closer children were to their fathers, the less distressed and the happier they reported being.

10. Many couples struggle with differences over parenting, housework, sexual interest, and communication. I have chosen to focus my attention on married heterosexual couples because the bulk of the research has been done on this population. However, many of the ideas and recommendations made in this book would also be useful in gay and lesbian marriages/relationships, and unmarried, straight relationships. Further, most current research supports the idea that while some differences exist, gay and lesbian relationships are generally similar to straight relationships in terms of interaction and parenting behavior. See, for example, John Gottman's twelve-year study of gay and lesbian couples at www.gottman.com/research/projects/gaylesbian.

1: THE PERFECT MOTHER

1. According to an International Labor Organization report cited in Hochschild (1997, p. xxi).
2. Kozol (1992).
3. Ehrensaft (1997, p. 135) writes about middle-class families, "As parents sweep their children up in the same mania that governs their own lives, the children are so overcommitted and overscheduled that they could not possibly attend to all the tasks expected of them in a week . . . Parents, rather than being able to pull their children out of the rat race, try to compensate by taking over some of the child's load . . . But if the trade off is a few hours less sleep for a reduction of a child's stress and an enhancement of a child's success, the parents are all for it." See also Coltrane (1996, p. 26).
4. See Crittenden (2001).
5. Coltrane (1996, p. 26); Ehrensaft (1997).
6. Presser (2003). Hochschild (1989, p. 242) also observed that the increasing shift to a job culture has undermined the values necessary for the stability of families. In a more recent article, Hochschild (2002, p. 46) writes that during the past few years, we have harmed families through slashing funds for maternal and child health grants, class size reduction, early learning programs, emergency medical services for children, hospital insurance for the uninsured, newborn and infant hearing screening, and mental-health programs. See also Coontz (1992).
7. Ooms (2002, p. 27).
8. Ehrensaft (1997).
9. Coltrane (1996, p. 202).
10. Baumrind (1989).
11. Ehrensaft (1997, pp. 11–12) describes this as "The Peter Pan Syndrome."
12. Hetherington and Kelly (2002, p. 119), observed that noncustodial fathers in

divorce more often behave in a companionate rather than a parental manner with their children.

13. Crittenden (2001); Ehrensaft (1997); Hochschild (1989, 1997).
14. Putnam (2000).
15. See Lewis, Amini, and Lannon (2000).
16. Coleman (2003).
17. Sociologist Belsky (1994, p. 244) writes, "If he is happy with her (wife), he will be present enough to develop the two foundations of good parenting, a close tie to and a great knowledge of his child. But if he is unhappy with his wife, he will spend so much time outside the family that neither of those foundations will develop."
18. Thompson and Walker (1989, p. 861).
19. Belsky and Kelly (1994, p. 28). He also found that while fathers had fewer lows with becoming a new parent, they also had fewer highs than the mother.
20. Thompson and Walker (1989, p. 855).
21. Ibid. As the authors note, "The conditions of family work are related to women's psychological function but not to men's. Most men do not experience family work as a test of their worth; it is not their 'real' work."

    And Coltrane (1996, p. 230) writes, "Given the lack of respect accruing to women outside the home, families remain one of the few domains where women's knowledge and authority are accepted and women's activities celebrated."
22. See West and Fenstermaker (1993).
23. Thompson and Walker (1995, p. 850).
24. In Belsky and Kelly (1994, p. 134).
25. Coltrane (2000, p. 1209).
26. Coltrane (1996, p. 31).
27. Thompson and Walker (1995, p. 850).
28. Crittenden (2001, p. 74). She (ibid., p. 77) also notes that mothers who don't work outside the home, or who work part-time forfeit billions of dollars a year in retirement income because parenting and housework aren't counted as labor, and therefore don't earn Social Security credits.

    Anthropologist Sarah Hrdy (1999, p. 223) cautions that while women in the West, and the United States especially, have many opportunities to negotiate a more equal relationship with their spouses, the majority of women in other parts of the world, such as the Middle East, Asia, and North Africa, live in societies that are far more coercive and restrictive of their behavior. Women's disregard of men's thoughts and feelings, especially in the sexual domain, are more likely to get a woman killed or disfigured rather than advance her well-being or self-esteem.

29. Crittenden (2001, p. 46).

30. Ibid., p. 56.

31. Ibid., pp. 63–64. Currently, only California, Louisiana, and New Mexico grant a wife half of all marital assets in the case of divorce (2001, p. 32).

32. Index, *Harper's Magazine,* April 2004. From the U.S. General Accounting Office report entitled "Women's Earnings: Work Patterns Partially Explain Difference Between Men's and Women's Earnings," released on November 20, 2003. "When we account for differences between male and female work patterns as well as other key factors, women earned, on average, 80 percent of what men earned in 2000."

33. Mahony (1995, p. 76). Crittenden (2001, p. 35) writes on this topic, "With the arrival of a child, a mother's definition of accomplishment becomes more complex, her work load goes up, and her income and independence go down."

34. Gottman (1994). See also Cowan and Cowan (2000) and Belsky and Kelly (1994).

35. Hochschild (1989, p. 53) refers to this as the "politics of comparison"—the notion that people consciously or unconsciously make determinations about what is fair to do or demand from another, based on the "going rate" for a particular behavior. Thompson and Walker (1995, p. 850) observe that part of what causes many women to feel overwhelmed is their inability to recognize the inherent unfairness in the distribution of family labor.

36. Belsky and Kelly (1994, p. 28).

37. Hochschild (1989, p. 214) writes, "Because changing economic opportunities and needs influence women more powerfully than men, women differ more from their mothers than men differ from their fathers. . . . More importantly, things at home have changed much less than women's feelings have changed about forging some kind of identity at work."

38. Ibid., p. 234.

39. Allen and Hawkins (1999, pp. 202–203).

40. Ibid., p. 202.

41. In a study of egalitarian marriages, Haas (1980, p. 294) writes, "Not only did the wives have to contend with the husband's disinclination to do chores, they also had to cope with guilty feelings about abandoning their traditional role and with the mixed feelings they had seeing their husbands do non-traditional tasks."

42. Ibid. See also Belsky and Kelly (1994).

43. Allen and Hawkins (1999, p. 203); Hochschild (1989, p. 210).

2: CREATING CHANGE

1. Mahony (1995, p. 103).

2. Hrdy (1999, p. 137).

3. Ibid.; Mahony (1995).
4. Brown (1986), cited in Mahony (1995, p. 57).
5. Mahony (1995, p. 57).
6. I am especially indebted to Rhona Mahony for many of the ideas contained in this chapter.
7. Belsky and Kelly (1994, p. 28).
8. Coltrane (2000, p. 1221) reports the following: "Studies from the 1990's show that women's egalitarian gender ideology is a consistent predictor of household labor sharing. When wives feel more strongly that both paid work and family work should be shared and when they agree more fully with statements about equality between women and men, they are more likely to share housework with husbands. . . . In general, younger women do less housework and share more of it than do older women."
9. Hetherington and Kelly (2002, p. 41).
10. Mahony (1995, p. 95). Hochschild (1989, p. 189) speaks of a similar idea with her concept of the "sharing showdown," and Hood, cited in Coltrane (1996, p. 109), offers her advice that women in this situation should "go on strike."
11. See Bourne (2000).
12. Allen and Hawkins (1999, p. 203).
13. Mahony (1995, p. 96).
14. See Hackstaff (1999).
15. Crittenden (2001, p. 199).
16. Ibid., p. 199.
17. Ibid., p. 77.
18. Finley. www.dadsdivorce.com/mag/essay.php/1017Father.html.
19. Coltrane (2000, p. 1220).

3: ONCE CHILDREN ARRIVE

1. Hetherington and Kelly (2002, p. 25). See also Belsky and Kelly (1994); Cowan and Cowan (1992); Gottman (1994).
2. Cowan and Cowan (1992, p. 189).
3. Ibid.; Belsky and Kelly (1994).
4. Belsky and Kelly (1994, p. 109).
5. Ibid., p. 28.
6. *Psychology Today,* 2003.
7. Belsky and Kelly (1994, p. 27).
8. Ibid., pp. 228–9.
9. Reiss (1995).
10. Pruett (2000).
11. Hochschild (1989, p. 4).

12. Belsky and Kelly (1994, p. 33).
13. Mahony (1995, p. 106).
14. Ibid.
15. Belsky and Kelly (1994, p. 33).
16. Mahony (1995, p. 213).
17. Coltrane (1996, p. 144).
18. Ehrensaft (1997, p. 135).
19. Gottman (1994).
20. Ibid.
21. Belsky and Kelly (1994, p. 28).
22. Ibid.
23. See Hetherington and Kelly (2002); Gottman (1994).
24. Belsky and Kelly (1994, p. 40).
25. Ibid., p. 99; Gottman (1994).
26. Belsky and Kelly (1994, p. 199).
27. Ibid., p. 28.
28. Gottman (1994).
29. Hochschild (1989, p. 19).
30. Hetherington and Kelly (2002); Amato and Booth (1997); Gottman (1994).

4: FOUNDATIONS: WHAT KIND OF MARRIAGE DO I HAVE?

1. Coltrane (1996, p. 205); Belsky (1994, p. 141). Hochschild (1989, p. 209) found that most of the men she studied were "transitional in gender ideology and resistant in strategy."
2. I've chosen these categories to be consistent with how these arrangements are represented in the research literature.
3. See Lakoff (2002).
4. Hochschild (1989); Belsky and Kelly (1994).
5. Many have written on this topic. In addition to others listed so far, see Deutsch (2000); Ehrensaft (1987); Risman (1999).
6. Mahony (1995, p. 80).
7. As Belsky and Kelly (1994, p. 143) write, "Putting a high priority on domesticity, the traditional wife wants and expects to assume the lion's share of the chores."
8. Ibid., p. 144.
9. Hochschild (1989, p. 75).
10. Ibid.
11. Belsky and Kelly (1994, p. 143).

12. Crittenden (2001); Mahony (1995); Coltrane (2000).
13. Mahony (1995).
14. Hochschild (1989, p. 210).
15. Belsky and Kelly (1994, p. 141) write, "In our study we found the transitional marriage to be the most common form of ideological matchup, as I suspect it is in the general population." However, "Typically transitional couples have as much trouble with division of labor and work issues as husbands and wives in ideologically mixed marriages. Why? One virtue of being at either end of the ideological spectrum is the clarity it confers."
16. Ibid., p. 116.
17. Allen and Hawkins's study (1999) was cited in Slonaker (2003).
18. Belsky and Kelly (1994).
19. Haas (1980, p. 293).
20. Ibid., p. 294.
21. Daniels and Weingarten (1988), in Bronstein and Cowan, eds., (1988).
22. Gottman (1994, p. 160) observes that most marriages don't end because of out-of-control conflicts, but rather the ongoing avoidance of it.
23. Hochschild (1989, p. 189).
24. Gottman (1994, p. 109).
25. Belsky and Kelly (1994).
26. Hochschild (1989).
27. See Fisher (1992); Hetherington and Kelly (2002).
28. Huber and Spitze (1983), cited in Hochschild (1989, p. 224), showed that the more housework a husband did, the less his wife thought about divorce. They found that if a working wife believes that her husband should share housework, she is 10 percent more likely to have thoughts of divorce than if she doesn't believe this.
29. Belsky and Kelly (1994).
30. Hochschild (1989, p. 232).
31. Coltrane (1996, p. 112); Hochschild (1989).
32. Belsky and Kelly (1994, p. 137).
33. Cowan and Cowan (1992, p. 203).

5: CHILDHOOD REVISITED

1. There is a lot of data to support the notion that conflict in marriage is handed down over the generations. For reviews, see Amato (1994); Amato and Booth (1997); Dadds, Atkinson, Turner, Blums, and Lendich (1999); Grych and Fincham, (1990); Kelly (2000); Morrison and Coiro (1999).
2. Fraiberg (1980).

3. Thompson and Walker (1989, p. 863).
4. Weiss (1993).

6: IT'S A PERSONALITY THING

1. Two good self-help books on this topic are Page (1997), and Young and Klosko (1994).
2. Cross and Madson (1997); Kiecolt-Glaser and Newton (2001).
3. American Psychiatric Association (2000), Diagnostic and statistical manual of mental disorders (DSM-IV).
4. Heriot and Pritchard (2004).
5. Nolen-Hoeksema, Larson, and Grayson (1999); Nolen-Hoeksema and Girgus (1994).
6. Cross and Madson (1997).
7. DSM-IV (2000).
8. Young and Klosko (1994, pp. 294–313).
9. Haring and Hewitt (2003, p. 23).
10. Ibid.
11. Schaefer and Burnett (1987); Ptacek and Dodge (1995).
12. Gottman (1994).
13. Gottman (1994, p. 84) found that distressed couples commonly underestimate the other's positive contributions by as much 50 percent.
14. Flett and Hewitt (2002).
15. Ibid.
16. See Forward (1987, 1997).
17. Nelson (2001).
18. The following are some guidelines if you live with domestic violence cited from Coleman (2004):

   ➤ Develop a safety plan. This means that if you have to rush out of the door with your kids, you have a definite place that you can stay, with a person you trust. You should also leave changes of clothes there for you and your children along with money.
   ➤ Assess your partner's willingness to change by suggesting he get into a batterer's intervention program.
   ➤ Begin with small changes in yourself such as slowly increasing your assertiveness and independence. The task is to develop yourself without acting or feeling like a victim in the marriage. Use the techniques recommended for working with verbal abuse, though you may need to go more slowly. Your safety is the top priority.
   ➤ Call the National Domestic Violence/Abuse Hotline: 800-799-

SAFE (800-799-7233). Callers can be given immediate directions and assistance, including emergency shelters, referrals, counseling, and reporting abuse.

➤ Web site: SAFE, Stop Abuse for Everyone, http://www.safe4all.org Comprehensive list of Web resources, local shelters, and personal stories of others who have lived with domestic violence. Useful for both women and men.

Center for the Prevention of Sexual and Domestic Violence: 206-634-1903
National Coalition Against Domestic Violence: 703-765-0339
19. Forward (1987, 1997).
20. Kierkegaard (1959).
21. Black (1981).
22. Bourne (2000).
23. Ibid.
24. Forward (1987; 1997); Nelson (2001).
25. Coleman (2004); Dadds, Atkinson, Turner, Blums, and Lendich (1999).
26. Gottman (1994).
27. Forward (1987; 1997); Nelson (2001).
28. Ibid.
29. Gottman (1994, p. 84).

7: WHAT'S WITH MEN, ANYWAY?

1. Cashman (1995). Written under the pseudonym, Dr. Alan Francis.
2. Hawkins and Roberts (1992).
3. Crittenden (2001).
4. Coltrane (1996). Also read Coltrane (ibid., pp. 28–50) for an excellent historical review of how men's roles and the definition of masculinity have changed over the past few centuries. For example, he (ibid., p. 32) writes, "In Europe and America, before the nineteenth century, child rearing was also a more collective or communal enterprise. The entire community participated in virtually every aspect of an individual's life, including most of those things we now consider private family matters. In this older and more collective pattern, parent-child relations were constantly regulated and monitored by relatives and other community members and what happened inside the home was relatively public. . . . The home—previously the normal site of production, consumption, and virtually everything else in life—was slowly transformed into the only 'proper' place to find emotional security and release. . . . Under the previous agricultural economy the community regulated most family functions and repaired any moral defects of families.

In the newer industrial model, however, families and especially mothers were supposed to compensate for the moral defects of the larger society."

5. Crittenden (2001, p. 99).
6. Hawkins and Roberts (1992).
7. Anthropologist Sara Hrdy (1999) observed that men in some hunter-gatherer tribes give a large percentage of the meat that they kill to other families, rather than to their own wives and children. She reasoned that this was because men who gave it away increased their chances of sexual favors with potential future sex partners, and also increased their status among other men.
8. Pinker (2003, p. 329).
9. For reviews, see Baron-Cohen (2002, 2003), Pinker (2003), Tannen (1990).
10. Charlesworth and Dzur (1987).
11. Ibid.
12. Zahn-Waxler, Radke-Yarrow, Wagner, and Chapman (1992); Hoffman (1977).
13. Ahlgren and Johnson (1979).
14. Vuchinich (1987).
15. Tannen (1990, p. 154).
16. Baron-Cohen (2002, p. 90).
17. Glenn (1987). See also Mahony (1995); Coltrane (1996).
18. Diamond (1997). See also Hrdy (1999); Fisher (1992).
19. Ibid.
20. Hrdy (1999, p. 111).
21. Crittenden (2001, p. 120).
22. Ibid, p. 122; Hrdy (1999, p. 230).
23. Hrdy (1999, p. 10) writes, "Mothers evolved not to produce as many children as they could, but to trade off quantity for quality . . . and in that way increase the chance that at least a few offspring will survive and prosper."

She (ibid., p. 278) also writes, "Every human mother's response to her infant is influenced by a composite of biological repsonses of mammalian, primate, and human origin. These include endocrinal priming during pregnancy, physical changes including changes in the brain during and after birth; the complex feedback loops of lactations; and the cognitive mechanisms that enhance the likelihood of recognizing and learning to prefer kind. But almost none of these biological responses are automatic."

This biological difference may also affect who women choose as potential partners. Marital researchers, Hetherington and Kelly (2002, p. 24) observe that women tend to be more cautious and conservative when getting involved with a man. "Women approach love as informed consumers; metaphorically speaking, they kick the tires, look under the hood, run the motor, and check the mileage. Women love love; but being practical-minded, not enough to ignore potential defects . . . Despite a reputation for practicality, males come off as hopeless romantics . . . If the bodywork is good and the grille pretty, often a man will buy on the spot, no questions asked."

24. Hrdy (1999).
25. Fisher (1992, p. 77).
26. Coltrane (1996) in Crittenden (2001, p. 129).
27. Crittenden (2001).
28. Henneck (2003).
29. In addition to the authors mentioned thus far, see Cross and Madson (1997).
30. Tannen (1990, p. 152).
31. Baron-Cohen (2003, p. 37).
32. Ibid., p. 41.
33. Ibid., p. 29.
34. Tannen (1990, p. 177).
35. Goethals, Messick, and Allison (1991).
36. Tannen (1990); Baron-Cohen (2003); Cross and Madson (1997).
37. Cross and Madson (1997).
38. Tannen (1990, p. 128).
39. As Tannen (1990, p. 208) writes, ". . . claims that men dominate women because they interrupt them in conversation accept the assumption that conversation is an enterprise in which only one voice should be heard at a time. This erroneous assumption has significant consequences for women . . . But in the male-female constellation, it is women who are at a social and cultural disadvantage."
40. Tannen (1990); Baron-Cohen (2003); Cross and Madson (1997).
41. Maltz and Borker (1982).
42. Baron-Cohen (2003, p. 100).
43. Hammen and Peters (1978).
44. Hochschild (1989).
45. Tannen (1990).
46. Another perspective on this gender difference is presented by psychoanalyst Nancy Choderow (1978). She writes that a boy's sense of self is developed in part, by seeing himself as different from his mother, while a girl's identity is developed by seeing herself as similar. Boys, like girls, have historically been raised primarily by women. This means that while a girl gains her identity from experiencing herself as being like her mom, a boy gains his identity, in part by resisting that pull, and seeing himself as "not like mom." This means repudiating all that is feminine. So behaviors that are more often defined as feminine such as emotional expressiveness, affection, talking about feelings, etc., are disavowed because they're too much of a reminder of how a mother behaves.

As Choderow (ibid., p. 182) writes, "A boy's contempt serves to free him not only from his mother but also from the feminity within himself," what Freud referred to as "the normal male contempt for women." An aspect of boys' and men's commonly observed contempt for women can be understood through this lens. Most men and women have had too much of mother and not enough of father. Men's frequently observed desire for less time with their partners is an attempt to fight the pull of merging with her in the way that they felt merged with their own mothers. Women, who rarely got too much of father, are free to pursue closeness with a man without fear of getting more than they'd like. In other words, seeing women, and what women do as inferior is an attempt to distance themselves from this pull. This is different from a simple claim to be above housework and diaper changing; it's an attempt to maintain a sense of self.

Coltrane (1996, p. 35) observes that views about women's inferiority have increased historically when women have made gains in legal and economic arenas. This resistance may similarly stem from men's anxiety about women having equal or greater power. Boys are less likely to see women as inferior when they have more time with dad, and when they participate in activities with dad that have been more traditionally done by women.

47. Pruett (2000).
48. Coltrane (1996, p. 79).
49. Coltrane (2000); Hochschild (1989).
50. Allen and Hawkins (1999).
51. Ibid.
52. Belsky and Kelly (1994, p. 36).
53. Hochschild (1989) describes this as the "economy of gratitude."
54. Crittenden (2001).
55. Mahony (1995).
56. Skinner (1976).
57. Ibid.
58. Rock (1999).
59. Hetherington and Kelly (2002); Gottman (1994).
60. In Hrdy (1999, p. 223).
61. See Fisher (1992).
62. Thompson and Walker (1989).
63. Weiner-Davis (2003).
64. Gottman (1994).
65. Pittman (1999).
66. Weiner-Davis (2003).
67. Ibid.
68. Coleman (2001). Postpartum Depression. *TWINS Magazine,* May–June.

8: FOR THE HUSBAND

1. Gottman (1994).
2. Hetherington and Kelly (2002); Gottman (1994).
3. Gottman (1994, p. 155).
4. Ibid.
5. Kelly (2000).
6. Hendrix (1988).
7. Coltrane and Adams, cited in Lovekin (2003).
8. Amato and Booth (1997).
9. Hochschild (1989).
10. Gottman (1994). See his discussion of "harsh start-ups."
11. Stuart Smalley was a character developed by Al Franken for *Saturday Night Live*.
12. Gottman (1994).
13. Ibid.
14. Hetherington and Kelly (2002).

9: THE LAZY HUSBAND CAMPAIGN

1. Coltrane (1996, p. 202).
2. Ibid.
3. Mahony (1995).
4. Lubano (2004).
5. Coltrane (2000) and Adams, cited in Lovekin (2003). Coltrane (2000) notes that younger men are more likely these days to say that they enjoy and participate in cooking and cleaning.
6. Ibid.

References

Ahlgren, A., and D. W. Johnson. (1979). Sex differences in cooperative and competitive attitudes from the 2nd to the 12th grades. *Developmental Psychology* 15:45–49.

Allen, Sarah M., and Allen J. Hawkins. (1999). Maternal gatekeeping: Mothers' beliefs and behaviors that inhibit greater father involvement in family work. *Journal of Marriage and the Family* 61:199–212.

Amato, Paul R. (1994). Father-child relations, mother-child relations, and offspring psychological well-being in early adulthood. *Journal of Marriage and the Family* 56:1031–1042.

———. (1994). Life-span adjustment of children to their parents' divorce. *Future Child* 4:143–164.

Amato, Paul R., and Alan Booth. (1997). *A Generation at Risk*. Cambridge, MA: Harvard University Press.

American Psychiatric Association. *Diagnostic and statistical manual of mental disorders: DSM-IV-TR.* 4th ed. Washington, DC.

Baron-Cohen, Simon. (2002). The extreme male brain theory of autism. *Trends in Cognitive Sciences* 6(6).

———. (2003). *The Essential Difference: The Truth About the Male and Female Brain.* New York: Basic Books.

Baumrind, D. (1989). Rearing competent children. In *Child development today and tomorrow,* ed., W. Damon, pp. 349–378. San Francisco: Jossey-Bass.

Belsky, Jay, and John Kelly. (1994). *The Transition to Parenthood: How a First Child Changes a Marriage. Why Some Couples Grow Closer Together and Others Apart.* New York: Dell.

Bird, C. E. (1999). Gender, household, and psychological disease: The impact of the amount and division of housework. *Journal of Health and Social behavior,* 40:32–45.

Black, Claudia. (1981). *It Will Never Happen to Me.* New York: Ballantine Books.

Bourne, Edmund J. (2000). *The Anxiety and Phobia Workbook.* Oakland: New Harbinger Publications.

Brown, Roger. (1986). *Social Psychology.* 2nd ed. New York: Free Press.

Cashman, Cindy [Alan Francis, pseud.]. (1995). *Everything Men Know About Women.* Los Angeles: Andrews McNeel Publishing.

Charlesworth, W. R., and C. Dzur. (1987). Gender comparisons of preschoolers' behavior and resource utilization in group problem-solving. *Child Development* 58:191–200.

Choderow, Nancy. (1978). *The Reproduction of Mothering: Psychoanalysis and the Sociology of Gender.* Berkeley: University of California Press.

Coleman, Joshua. (2001). Postpartum depression. *TWINS Magazine,* May–June.

———. (2003). Married with twins. *TWINS Magazine,* July–August.

———. (2004). *The Marriage Makeover: Finding Happiness in Imperfect Harmony.* New York: St. Martin's Press.

Coltrane, Scott. (1996). *Family Man: Fatherhood, Housework, and Gender Equity.* New York: Oxford University Press.

———. (2000). Research on household labor: Modeling and measuring the social embeddedness of routine family work. *Journal of Marriage and the Family* 62:1208–1233.

Coontz, Stephanie. (1992). *The Way We Never Were.* New York: Basic Books.

Cowan, Carolyn, P., and Philip A. Cowan. (1989). Parents work patterns, marital and parent-child relationships and early child development. Paper presented at the meetings of the Society for Research in Child Development, Toronto, Canada. Cited in Hochschild. (1989)

———. (1992). *When Partners Become Parents.* New York: Basic Books.

Crittenden, Ann. (2001). *The Price of Motherhood: Why the Most Important Job in the World Is Still the Least Valued.* New York: Henry Holt.

Cross, S. E., and L. Madson. (1997). Models of the self: Self-construals and gender. *Psychological Bulletin* 1222(1):5–37.

Dadds, M. R., E. Atkinson, C. Turner, G. J. Blums, and B. Lendich. (1999). Family conflict and child adjustment: Evidence for a cognitive contextual model of intergenerational transmission. *Journal of Family Psychology* 13:194–208.

Daniels, P., and K. Weingarten. (1988). The fatherhood click: The timing of parenthood in men's lives. In ed., *Fatherhood Today: Men's Changing Role in the Family,* Phylis Bronstein and Carolyn P. Cowan, pp. 36–52. New York: John Wiley.

Deutsch, Francine. (2000). *Halving It All: How Equally Shared Parenting Works.* Cambridge, MA: Harvard.

Diamond, Jared. (1997). *Why Is Sex Fun? The Evolution of Human Sexuality.* New York: Basic Books.

Ehrensaft, Diane. (1997). *Spoiling Childhood: How Well-meaning Parents Are Giving Children Too Much—But Not What They Need.* New York: The Guilford Press.

————. (1987). *Parenting Together*. New York: Free Press.

Finley, G. www.dadsdivorce.com/mag/essay.php/1017Father.html.

Fisher, Helen. 1992. *Anatomy of Love: The Natural History of Monogamy, Adultery, and Divorce*. London: Simon & Schuster.

Flett, G. L., and P. L. Hewitt. 2002. *Perfectionism: Theory, research and treatment*. Washington, DC: American Psychological Association.

Forward, Susan. (1987). *Men Who Hate Women and the Women Who Love Them*. New York: Bantam Books.

————. (1997). *Emotional Blackmail: When the People in Your Life Use Fear, Obligation, and Guilt to Manipulate You*. New York: HarperPerennial.

Fraiberg, Selma. (1980). Ghosts in the nursery. In *Clinical studies of Infant Mental Health*, ed., S. Fraiberg. New York: Basic Books.

Glenn, E. N. (1987). Gender and the family. In *Analyzing Gender: A Handbook of Social Science Research*, ed., Beth B. Hess and Myra M. Ferree, pp. 348–360. Newbury Park, CA: Sage.

Goethals, G., D. M. Messick, and S. T. Allison. (1991). The uniqueness bias: Studies of Constructive social comparison. In *Social Comparison: Contemporary Theory and Research*, ed., J. Suls and T. A. Wills. Hillsdale, NJ: Erlbaum.

Gottman, John. (1994). *Why Marriages Succeed or Fail . . . And How You Can Make Yours Last*. New York: Simon & Schuster.

Grych, John H., and Frank D. Fincham. (1990). Marital conflict and children's adjustment: A cognitive contextual framework. *Psychological Bulletin* 108: 267–290.

Haas, Linda. (1980). Role-sharing couples: A study of egalitarian marriages. *Family Relations* 29:289–296.

Hackstaff, K. B. (1999). *Marriage in a Culture of Divorce*. Philadephia: Temple University Press.

Hammen, C. I., and S. D. Peters. (1978). Interpersonal consequences of depression: Responses to men and women enacting a depressed role. *Journal of Abnormal Psychology* 87:322–332.

Haring, M., and P. L. Hewitt. (2003). Perfectionism, coping, and quality of intimate relationships, *Journal of Marriage and the Family* 65(1):143–158.

Hawkins, A. J., T. A. Roberts. (1992). Designing a primary intervention to help dual-earner couples share housework and child care. *Family Relations* 41:169–177.

Hendrix, Harville. (1988). *Getting the Love You Want: A Guide for Couples*. New York, HarperPerennial.

Henneck, R. (2003). Family policy in the US, Japan, Germany, Italy and France: Parental leave, child benefits/family allowance, child care, marriage/cohabitation, and divorce. Briefing paper prepared for the Council on Contemporary Families, www.contemporaryfamilies.org/public/articles.

Heriot, S. A., and M. Pritchard. (2004). Test of time: "Reciprocal inhibition as the main basis of psychotherapeutic effects" by Joseph Wolpe (1954). *Clinical Child Psychology and Psychiatry* 9(2):297–307.

Hetherington, E. Mavis, and John Kelly. (2002). *For Better or for Worse: Divorce Reconsidered*. New York: W. W. Norton.

Hoffman, M. L. (1977). Sex differences in empathy and related behaviors. *Psychological Bulletin* 84:712–722.

Hochschild, Arlie. (1989). *The Second Shift: Working Parents and the Revolution at Home*. New York: Viking.

———. (1997). *The Time Bind: When Work Becomes Home and Home Becomes Work*. New York: Henry Holt.

———. (2002). Taking care. *The American Prospect* 13(7) April 8.

Hrdy, Sara Blaffer. (1999). *Mother Nature: Maternal Instincts and How They Shape the Human Species*. New York: Ballantine Books.

Huber, J., and G. Spitze. (1983). Sex stratification: Children, housework, and jobs. New York: Academic Press. Cited in Hochschild (1989).

Jasso, G., and P. H. Rossi. (1977). "Distributive justice and earned income." *American Sociological Review* 42:639–651.

Kelly, Joan B. (2000). Children's adjustment in conflicted marriage and divorce: A decade review of research. *Journal of the American Academy of Child and Adolescent Psychiatry* 39:8.

Kiecolt-Glaser, Janice K., and Tamara L. Newton. (2001). Marriage and health: His and hers. *Psychological Bulletin,* 127:472–503.

Kierkegaard, Soren. (1959). The rotation method: An essay in the theory of social prudence. Vol. 1 of *Either / Or*. Princeton: Princeton University Press, 279–296.

Kozol, Jonathan. (1992). *Savage Inequalities: Children in America's Schools*. New York: Perennial.

Lakoff, George. (2002). *Moral Politics: How Liberals and Conservatives Think*. Chicago: University of Chicago Press.

Lewis, Thomas, Fari Amini, and Richard Lannon. (2000). *A General Theory of Love*. New York: Random House.

Lovekin, Kris. (2003). When dads clean house, it pays off big time. UC Riverside sociologists say men likely to have better behaved children and wives who find them more sexually attractive. *Brain and Behavioural Sciences* no. 98, (June 8).

Lubano, A. (2004). Dad just keeps bumbling along: Dolts are alive, if not well, in TV Ads. *Philadelphia Inquirer,* April 10.

Mahony, Rhona. (1995). *Kidding Ourselves: Breadwinning, Babies, and Bargaining Power*. New York: Basic Books.

Maltz, D., and R. A. Borker. (1982). A cultural approach to male-female mis-communications. In *Language and Social Identity,* ed. John J. Gumperz, pp. 196–216. Cambridge: Cambridge University Press.

Morrison, D. R., and M. J. Coiro. (1999). Parental conflict and marital disruption: Do children benefit when high conflict marriages are dissolved? *Journal of Marriage and the Family* 61:626–637.

Nelson, Noelle. (2001). *Dangerous Relationships: How to Identify and Respond to the Seven Warning Signs of a Troubled Relationship.* New York: Perseus.

Nolen-Hoeksema, S., J. Larson, and C. Grayson. (1999). Explaining the gender difference in depressive symptoms. *Journal of Personality and Social Psychology.*

Nolen-Hoeksema, S., and J. S. Girgus. (1994). The emergence of gender differences in depression during adolescence. *Psychological Bulletin* 115:424–443.

Ooms, Theodora. (2002). Marriage plus: Most people agree that it's healthy to grow up in a two-person family. But the marriage contract is just the beginning. *American Prospect,* April.

Page, Susan. (1997). *How One of You Can Bring the Two of You Together.* New York: Broadway Books.

Pina, D. L., and V. L. Bengston. (1993). The division of household labor and wives' happiness-Ideology, employment, and perceptions of support. *Journal of Marriage and the Family* 55:901–912.

Pinker, Stephen. (2003). *The Blank Slate: The Modern Denial of Human Nature.* New York: Viking.

Pittman, Frank. (1999). *Grow Up! How Taking Responsibility Can Make You a Happy Adult.* New York: St. Martin's Press.

Presser, H. B. (2003). *Working in a 24/7 Economy: Challenges for American Families.* New York: Russell Sage Foundation

Pruett, Kyle. (2000). *Fatherneed: Why Father Care Is as Essential as Mother Care for Your Child.* New York: Free Press.

Psychology Today. (2003). Night Life.

Ptacek, J. T., and K. L. Dodge. (1995). Coping strategies and relationship satisfaction in couples. *Personality and Social Psychology Bulletin* 21: 76–84.

Putnam, Robert D. (2000). *Bowling Alone: The Collapse and Revival of American Community.* New York: Simon & Schuster.

Radin, Norma, and Graeme Russell. (1982). Increased father participation and child development outcomes. In *Nontraditional Families: Parenting and Child Development,* ed. M. E. Lamb, Hillsdale, NJ.: Erlbaum.

Reiss, D. (1995). Genetic influence on family systems: Implications for development. *Journal of Marriage and the Family* 57:543–560.

Risman, Barbara. (1999). *Gender Vertigo: American Families in Transition.* New Haven, CT: University Press.

Rock, Chris. (1999). *Bigger and Blacker*. HBO Studios.

Schaefer, E. S., and C. K. Burnet. (1987). Stability and predictability of quality of women's marital relationships and demoralization. *Journal of Personality and Social Psychology* 53: 1129–1136.

Skinner, B. F. (1976). *About Behaviorism*. New York: Vintage Books.

Slonaker, L. (2003). If you want it done right . . . Why women still perform most of the housework, even as men are increasingly willing to do their share. *San Jose Mercury News,* August.

Tannen, Deborah. (1990). *You Just Don't Understand.* New York: Ballantine Books.

Thompson, L., and A. J. Walker. (1989). Gender in families: Women and men in marriage, work and parenthood. *Journal of Marriage and the Family* 57 (November):845–871.

Thompson, L., and A. J. Walker. (1995). The place of feminism in family studies. *Journal of Marriage and the Family* 57 (November):847–865.

Vuchinich, S. (1987). Starting and stopping spontaneous family conflicts. *Journal of Marriage and the Family* 49:591–601.

Weiner-Davis, Michele. (2003). *The Sex-Starved Marriage: A Couple's Guide to Boosting Their Marriage Libido.* New York: Simon & Schuster.

Weiss, Joseph. (1993). *How Psychotherapy Works: Process and Technique.* New York: The Guilford Press.

West, C., and S. Fenstermaker. (1993). Power and the accomplishment of gender. In *Theory on Gender/Feminism on Theory,* ed. P. England, pp. 151–174. New York: Aldine de Gruyter.

Young, Jeffrey E., and Janet S. Klosko. (1994). *Reinventing Your Life.* New York: Dutton.

Zahn-Waxler, C., M. Radke-Yarrow, E. Wagner, and M. Chapman. (1992). Development of concern for others. *Developmental Psychology* 28: 126–136.